HAL•LEONARD
BANJO PLAY-ALONG

VOL. 3

Folk Rock Hits

Recording credits:
Mike Schmidt – Banjo, Mike DeRose – Guitar, Steve Cohen – Ha̶̶̶̶̶̶̶̶ ̶̶̶̶̶̶̶̶cholson – Violin,
Jack Dune – Drums, Brian Myers – Piano, Chris Kringel – Bass, ̶̶̶̶̶̶̶̶truments and production

ISBN 978-1-4803-4535-5

HAL•LEONARD®
CORPORATION

7777 W. BLUEMOUND RD. P.O. BOX 13819 MILWAUKEE, WI 53213

For all works contained herein:
Unauthorized copying, arranging, adapting, recording, Internet posting, public performance, or other distribution
of the printed or recorded music in this publication is an infringement of copyright.
Infringers are liable under the law.

Visit Hal Leonard Online at
www.halleonard.com

Performance Notes
By Mike Schmidt

Thank you for purchasing this collection of folk/rock tunes for the 5-string banjo. I hope you enjoy this book and playing along with "the band." First of all, I would like to thank my editor, Jim Schustedt, for all his help, patience, and particularly, his ear. Transcribing from recordings is always challenging, and in some of these tunes, the banjo was often so far in the background that hearing exactly what was being played was difficult. When this happened, I'd send my notes to Jim, with lots of holes where I couldn't tell what was played; then he'd send them back with his suggestions. It was quite a process, but we got through it. Together, we've produced a good reference source for these tunes. Thanks also to Chris Kringel, who provided the backing tracks for every tune. His arrangements are spot on.

This is an upper-intermediate to advanced level book, so there are many things to keep in mind with these tunes, not the least of which is the variety of keys. For that reason, songs in this book will require a capo. On a 5-string banjo, that means you will need a 5th string capo as well. Don't worry, you can play the songs without a capo, but the accompanying audio tracks are in the same keys as the originals, so you will need one to "play along." There are a few choices for the 5th string capo, but I prefer, and highly recommend, the basic "model-railroad spike." This is nothing more than a few small nails, usually installed at the 7th, 9th, and 12th frets of the 5th string. They cost next to nothing, they're unobtrusive, easily installed, minimally invasive, and readily available at hobby shops that sell electric trains (and even at some music stores). This is not a project for the faint of heart or the owner of an expensive banjo, unless you have experience. Trust installation to a professional who has done this before. I suggest the larger "O" gauge spikes. The internet is full of instructions, but let it be known that this is your responsibility. I cannot tell you how to do it in this book nor can we be responsible for the results. At the risk of repetition, I strongly suggest hiring an experienced professional instrument repair person.

There are also slide-type capos that mount along the binding on the side of the neck. I don't care for these because they get in the way of your thumb, and they can leave nasty scars on the banjo if removed. The small holes left by the spikes, if removed, can be filled with a dab of wood putty and colored with a felt-tip marker.

On those tunes that use a capo, you will see two sets of accompaniment chord symbols above the staff. The ones in parentheses are relative to the capo, meaning that you're playing those chord positions. Those not in parentheses are the actual sounding chords that apply to vocals and other non-capoed instruments like mandolin and fiddle. As mentioned, the keys used for these tunes are those of the original recordings. This does not mean you are obliged to play them as such. There are a few considerations in determining the key. One is to play it in the key in which it was originally recorded. Another is the range of your vocalists. Yet another is the preference of the non-capoed instruments. So, once you learn the tune here and start playing with other people, feel free to experiment.

"Ain't It Enough"
Old Crow Medicine Show

A simple set of rolls in 3/4 time, there's nothing too tricky here except maybe the strums at the bottom of page 4 of the song. These are down strums, but you will notice that the arrows in the tablature point upward. This is the direction – in tab – of the strums, 4th through 1st string. So while physically it's a down strum, in tab the arrow points upward, corresponding to the ascending pitches. This will be described in more detail later in "Ho Hey."

"The Cave"
Mumford & Sons

A workout for your right hand, this consists largely of a series of repeated patterns. Learning a few one-measure patterns and repeating them will give you most of what you need to play the song.

Note that the entire first page of this tune consists of rests. While in the original the banjo is not played here, we included the chord symbols above the staves so that if you feel like improvising, you can see the direction the song is going.

There is a seven-measure multi-rest on line three. The progression here is the same as in the Intro, so if you should decide to play here, use that as a guide. Also notice the D.S. al Coda on the first page. This tells you to do something other than proceed straight through. If you are unfamiliar with this type of repeat, see the Banjo Notation Legend at the back of this book for particulars.

"Forget the Flowers"
Wilco

This song was a challenge, mainly because the majority of what was played on the original recording was most likely freeform improvising, and not always in a traditional bluegrass style. While we wrote it out note-for-note, only two sections are treated as solos, and therefore they are the sections to learn. The rest is accompaniment, so playing most anything that follows the chord progression is all you need to do. The two sections to really learn are the Banjo/Guitar Solo starting on page 3 of the song, and the Outro on the last page of the song. Note that both sections are mostly forward rolls, and are fretted mainly on the second string. In the Solo, that changes to a bit more fretting at the A chord, and in the Outro, it stays that way throughout.

"Ho Hey"
The Lumineers

This one is a bit of an exception in this collection, mainly because there is no banjo in the original recording. We found that there was a lot of interest in this tune, so we decided to arrange a banjo part for it. Think of it as a set of suggestions.

Since there is no right or wrong way to play this one, we started by letting the guitar play alone for the first four measures. Then, the banjo comes in. In the original, this is where the first Verse starts, so you could choose to hold off for another four measures.

The Intro and first Verse are basically strums, matching the guitar. Because of the feel of the song, I'd be tempted to remain silent until the Chorus, but if you play it as written, it builds nicely into the Chorus, getting bigger as the banjo switches to picking. Notice that the mandolin comes in at the Chorus, helping with that buildup.

In the Bridge, there's a quasi-frail pattern. It's a repeating right-hand motif starting with a simultaneous pick of the 1st and 2nd strings with the middle and index fingers. That's followed by a down-strum with the nails of the index, middle, and ring fingers (some or all), and finally a pick of the 5th string with the thumb. I think it really fits the feel of what's happening in the rest of the song at this point.

There's a lot of strumming in this one. As mentioned in "Ain't It Enough," notice the direction of the arrows. Down strums – those that are physically done from the top to bottom – are indicated by an "up" arrow in the tablature, and vise versa.

And speaking of strums, a downward strum (5th–1st) is done with the nails of the fingers, while an upward strum (1st–5th) is done with the nail of the thumb. When I do these strums, I try not to hit the strings with my picks. This is described in "Live and Die."

"Little Lion Man"
Mumford & Sons

The first consideration here is the tuning. This is capoed on the 3rd fret, but the 5th string is an open A note. So, capoed, the pitches (5th–1st) are A-F-Bb-D-F. It might be easier to tune the banjo normally without the capo, then install the capo, and finally raise the pitch of the 5th string to A.

While the banjo part in this tune is quite fast, it's not terribly complicated, so your main work here is in the right hand. A predominant roll is a variation on what I call a "thumb in-and-out" roll, starting at the Interlude. The interesting thing in this one is that the roll starts on the 5th string, so it's unconventional, the reverse of what you might be used to.

A lot of that thumb in-and-out roll is based on a D-position. There are two ways you might consider playing this. I believe that, whenever possible, it's best to use the original chord position. That said, I used a standard D-position with the index, middle, and pinky on the 3rd, 2nd, and 1st strings, respectively. For the Dsus4, I stretched the pinky up to the 5th fret (above the capo) of the first string. For the Bm chord, I left the original D-position there, but added the ring finger to the 4th fret of the 3rd string. I didn't lift the index. Again I stretched the pinky for the flatted 6th chord. Note that the open circles on the last two chord diagrams pertain to your index finger, which remains down, but is cancelled by the ring finger on the higher fret of that same string.

Standard D-Position

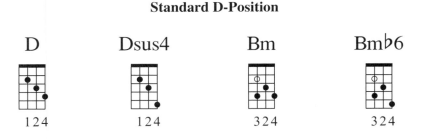

In the alternate position, you might do the D as shown below, with index, middle, and ring fingers, adding the pinky for the suspension. Then, the Bm could be done like an Am chord, again, adding the pinky for the flatted 6th. In the second and fourth chord diagrams below, the open circles represent your ring finger, which remains down. Personally, I prefer and recommend the first set.

Alternate D-Position

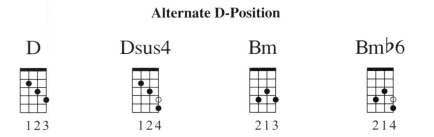

The most challenging aspect of the song is the Bridge. There's a long development part where the banjo repeats a four-beat pattern 28 times. In itself, it's not a difficult pattern, but repeating it that many times perfectly can be quite a task.

"Live and Die"
The Avett Brothers

This song is in the key of B. It's capoed on the 4th fret and played in a G-position, so the main chords you will be using are G, Bm, C, D, and Em. There are some interesting things happening in the right-hand. If you learned to play in a traditional bluegrass style, you'll see some rules being broken here, primarily the one where you're not supposed to use the same right-hand finger twice (or more) in a row unless there's a rest between them. The patterns are slow enough, however, that it's not difficult. In the first two lines, you will see several spots where you use the thumb as many as four times in a row.

Pay attention to the chords here. The Intro starts with a D-position (up the neck) I chord. The second is an up-the-neck Em position vi chord. Normally, you might do some kind of a barre chord, but seeing the previous chord is a D position, you can just move the middle finger from the 8th fret of the 2nd string down to the 7th fret and you'll get what you need. It saves lifting the entire chord and replacing it with something entirely different.

Something else to watch is the swing feel of the eighth notes. This is indicated by the parenthetical information to the right of the tempo marking on the first page of the song . The technique is to take each pair of eighth notes, lengthen the first, and shorten the second. This applies to hammer-ons as well.

Strumming: In a few spots, the banjo strums chords. Wearing finger picks, it's a conscious decision as to exactly how to strum. It requires both upstrokes and downstrokes. While you can just use the thumb pick for both directions, I do it differently and like the effect. I use the nails of my ring and pinky fingers of the right hand for the down strums, and the thumb pick for the up strums. This requires a bit more forearm and wrist motion than you may be used to, but it's also a nicer strum. Using two fingers without picks on them, you get a full strum because the fingers are different lengths. It's lighter than a downstroke with the thumb, as well. Then, since the thumb is a bit weaker on the upstroke, it matches the feel of those fingers used on the downstrokes. The hand shape is more-or-less like you're holding a ball loosely with the thumb, ring, and pinky fingers, with the index and middle held out straight to keep them out of the way.

"Switzerland"
The Last Bison

There are some interesting moves in this one. First of all, it's capoed on the 9th fret! Played in a G-position, that's the key of E, which is pretty high for the banjo. In this version, the 5th string is not played at all, so rather than tuning it all the way up to E, you might consider capoing the 5th string at the 9th fret with the rest of them, either with your 5th string capo or a guitar capo clamped across all five strings. That will make the pitch of the 5th string a B note, which is a chord tone of the E chord, if you should happen to hit it inadvertently.

Another complication with capoing so high is certain moves or chords can become a bit tricky because the frets are noticeably closer together. The initial riff is one such place. I found the 5th, 4th, 2nd fret movement on the first string challenging because my finger wanted to hit the 3rd fret when I was aiming for the 2nd.

Another spot is in the instrumental part where the Em chords are strummed. First, it's not a full Em; it's more of an Em7, in that only the 4th string is fretted at the 2nd fret. Typically I'd use my middle finger, but here it seems easier to use the index finger. This is even more apparent when you add the 2nd fret of the 3rd string a few times, using your middle finger. I found it was easier this way due to the narrow fret spacing.

"Wagon Wheel"
Old Crow Medicine Show

This is closer to a traditional 5-string style, but still with some variations.

As played on the original, the banjo player often lifts up his fret-hand fingers from chords and finishes the measure on open strings before changing to the next chord shape. This may be related to technique or ability.

In places where you see that second half played open, feel free to continue holding the chord to the end of that measure. If you need time to change chords, you might get away with playing the last note of the measure open rather than all four.

Eight measures into the second Fiddle Solo, there is a measure of triplets, all picked. So far, this has been mostly eighth notes, two per beat. All of a sudden, on this one measure, you need to pick three notes per beat. This happens at about 2:38 on the recording. Otherwise, it's pretty straightforward, save for some unusual right-hand patterns.

Enjoy!

Ain't It Enough

Words and Music by Ketch Secor, Jason White and Willie Watson

Key of C

Intro

Moderately fast ♩ = 160

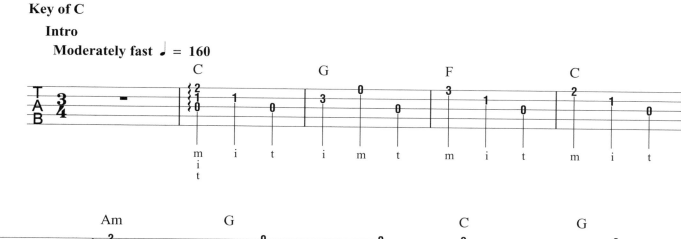

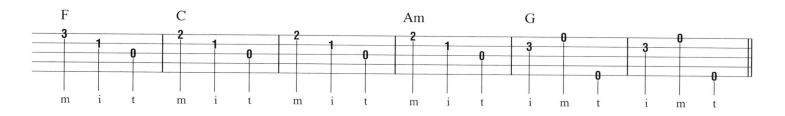

Verse

1. *Show me   a   river...*

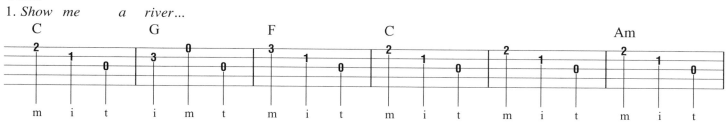

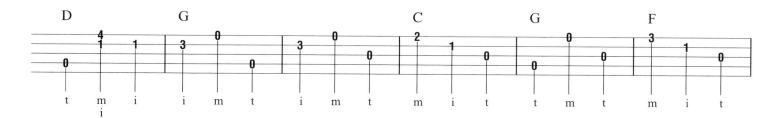

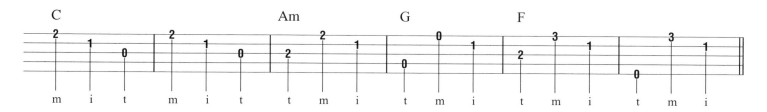

Copyright © 2012 Blood Donor Music, Broken Banjo Music, Hanging Vines and Better Angels Music
All Rights for Blood Donor Music and Broken Banjo Music Administered by Spirit One Music
International Copyright Secured   All Rights Reserved

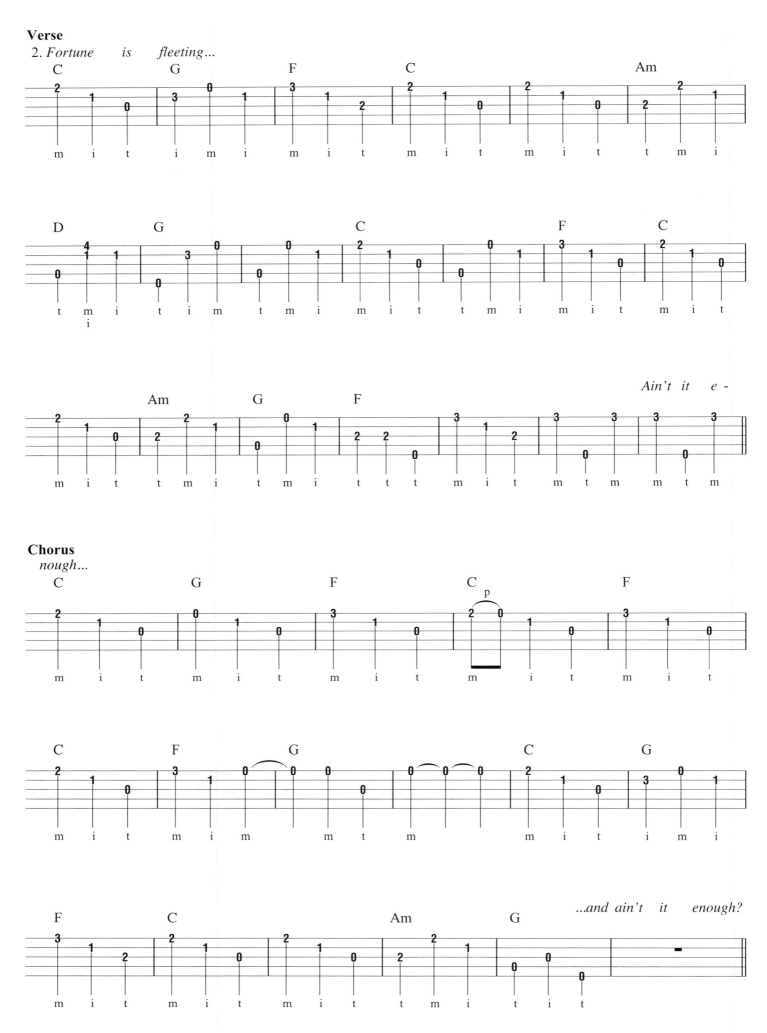

Harmonica Interlude

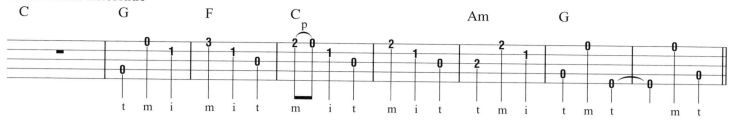

Verse

3. Surely all people...

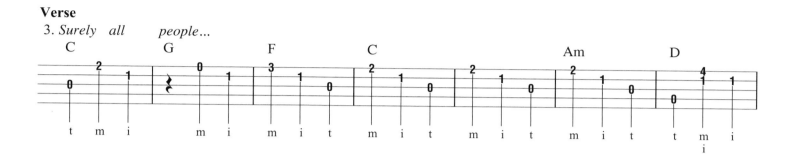

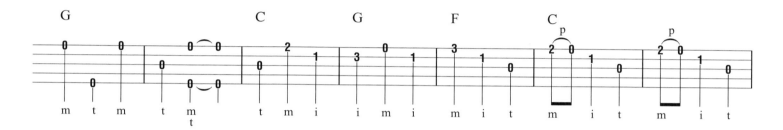

Ain't it e -

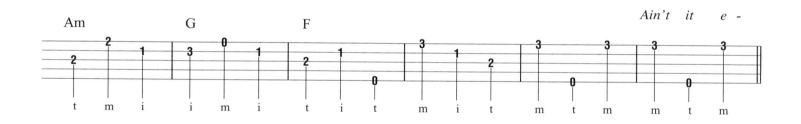

Chorus

nough...

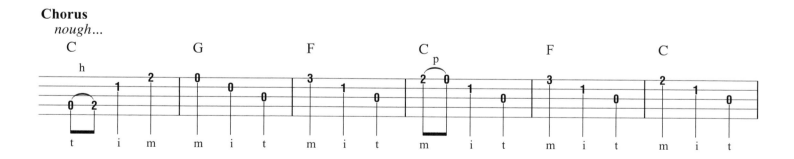

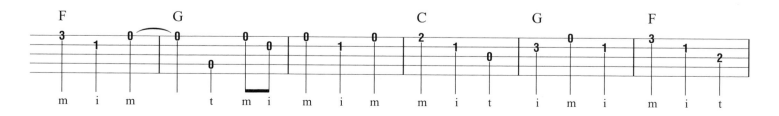

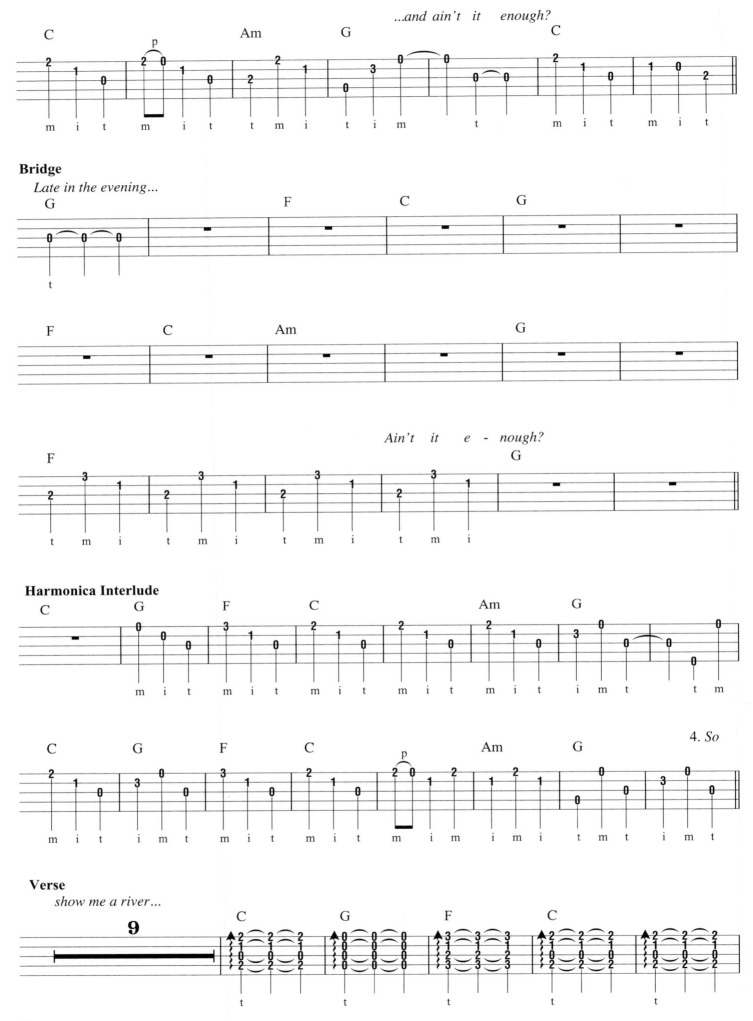

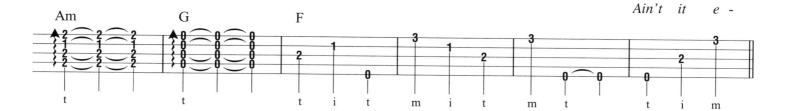

Ain't it e -

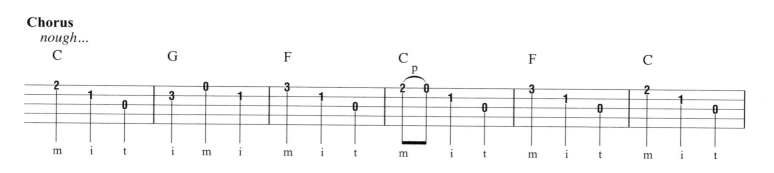

Chorus

nough...

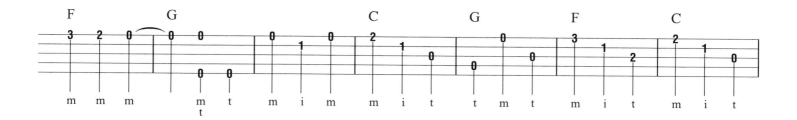

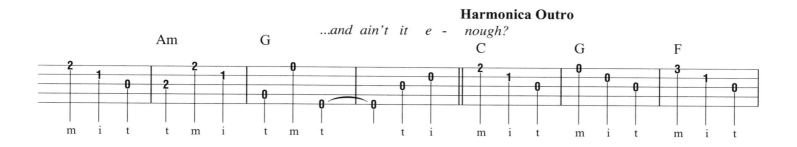

Harmonica Outro

...and ain't it e - nough?

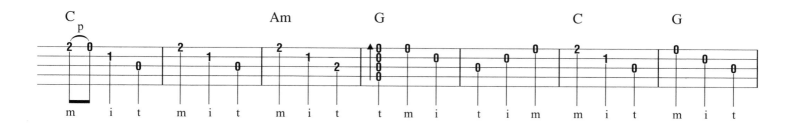

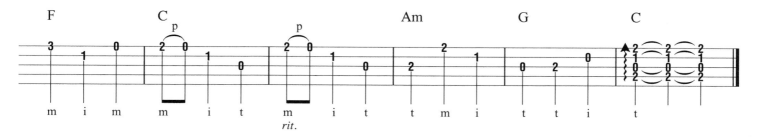

from Mumford & Sons - *Sigh No More*

The Cave

Words and Music by Mumford & Sons

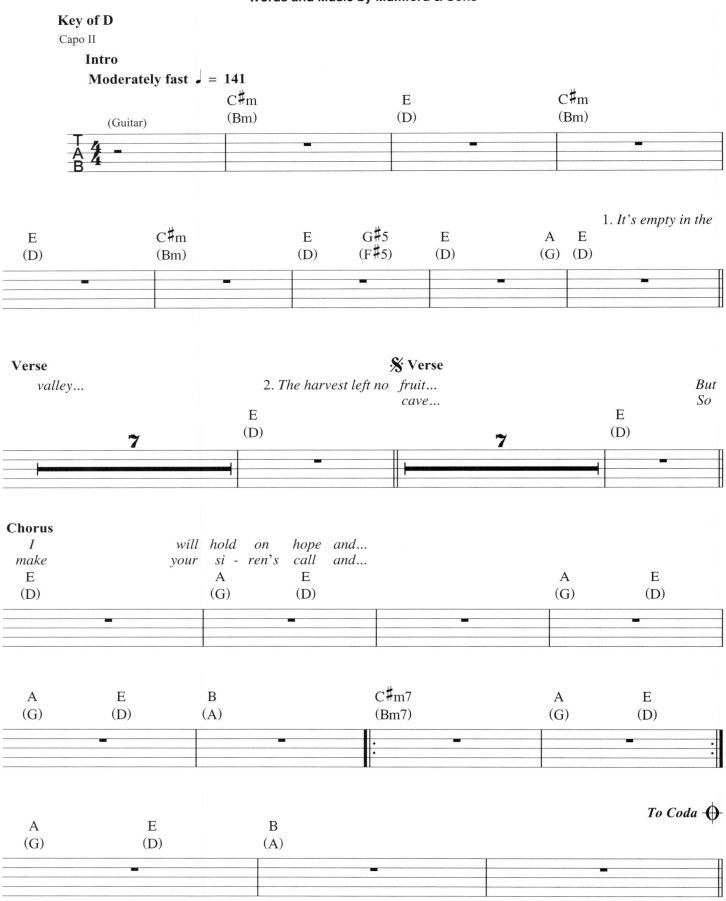

Copyright © 2009 UNIVERSAL MUSIC PUBLISHING LTD.
All Rights in the U.S. and Canada Controlled and Administered by UNIVERSAL - POLYGRAM INTERNATIONAL TUNES, INC.
All Rights Reserved   Used by Permission

Interlude

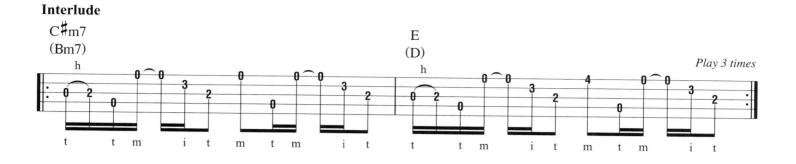

Play 3 times

3. 'Cause I have other

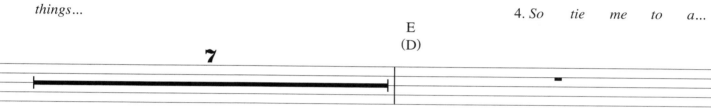

Verse

things...

4. *So   tie   me   to   a...*

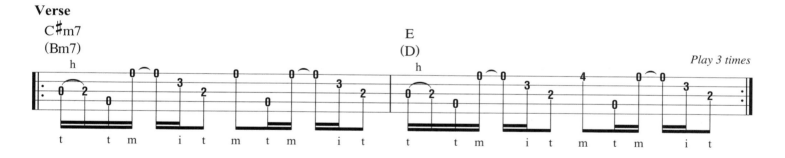

Verse

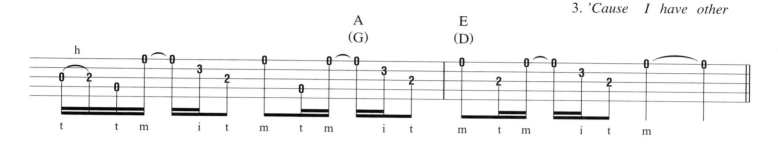

Play 3 times

But

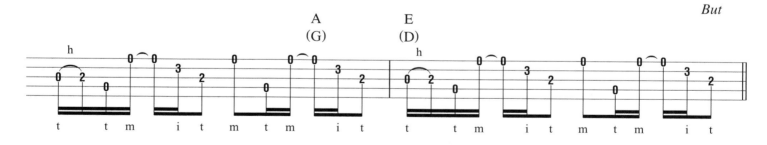

Chorus

I...

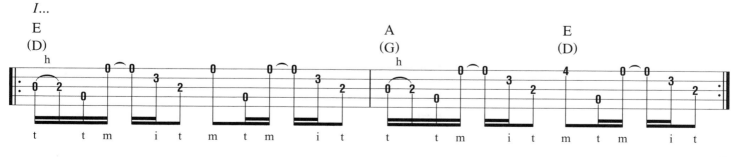

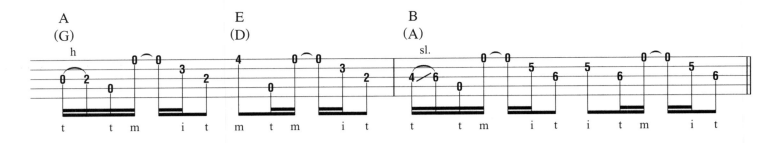

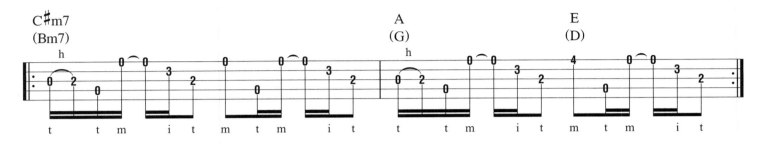

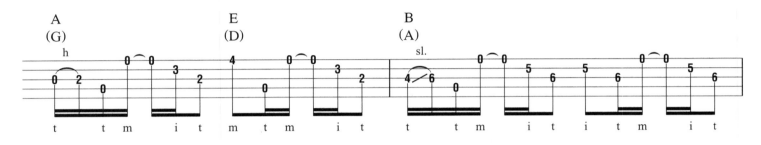

D.S. al Coda
(take repeats)

3. *So come out of your*

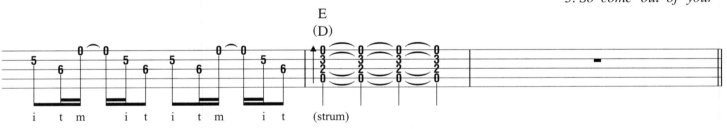

⊕ **Coda**
Interlude
Ah...

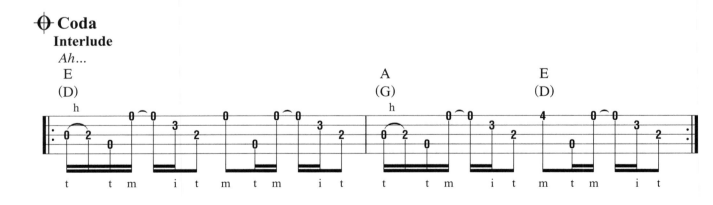

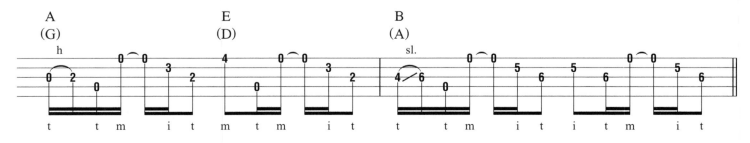

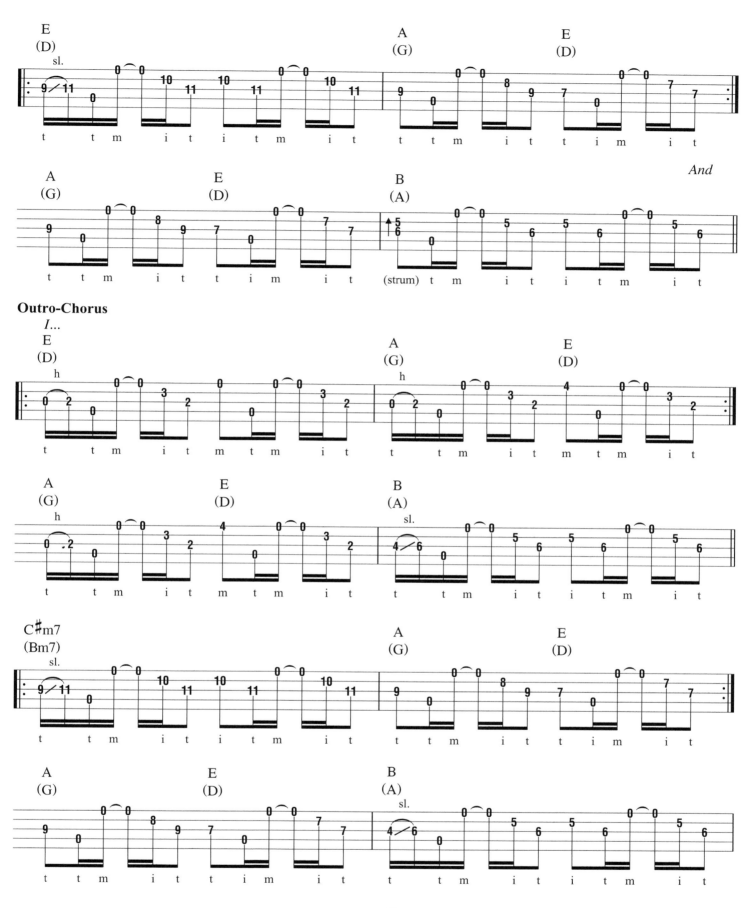

Outro-Chorus

I...

from Wilco - *Being There*

Forget the Flowers

Words and Music by Jeff Tweedy

Copyright © 1996 Words Ampersand Music
All Rights Administered by BMG Platinum Songs (US) LLC
All Rights Reserved   Used by Permission

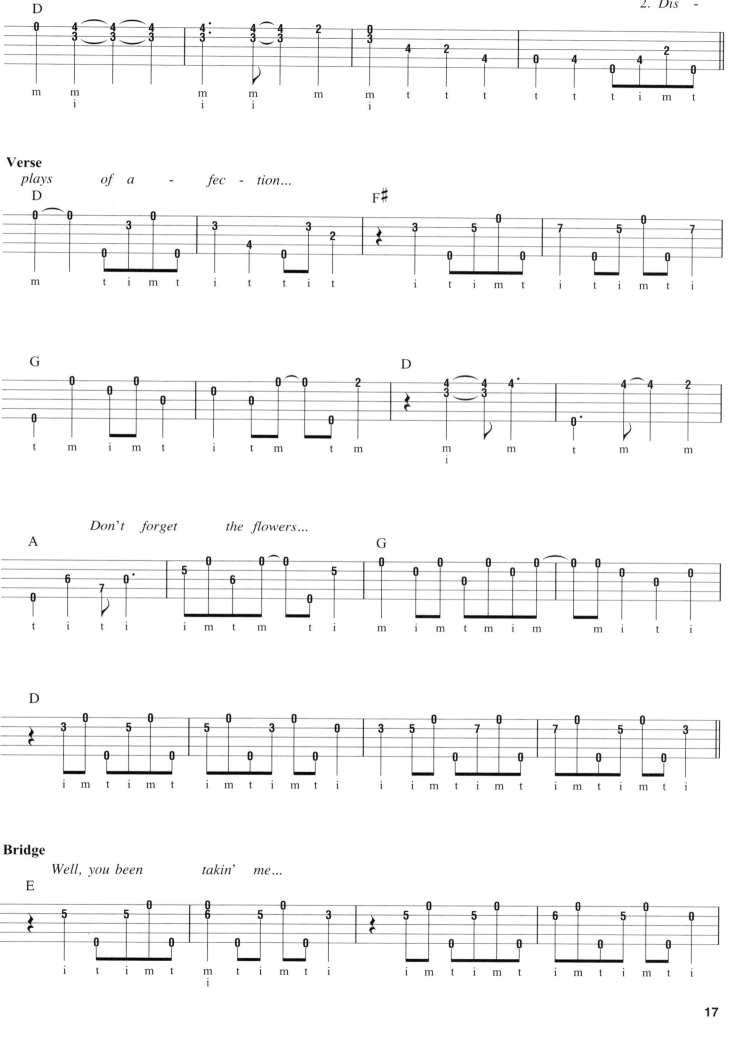

Verse

plays   of   a   -   fec - tion...

Don't   forget   the flowers...

Bridge

Well, you been   takin' me...

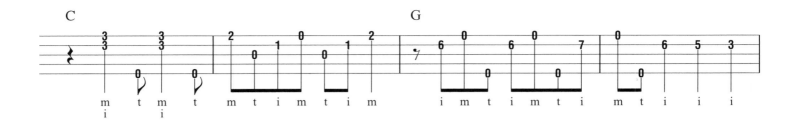

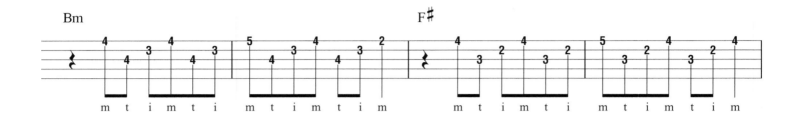

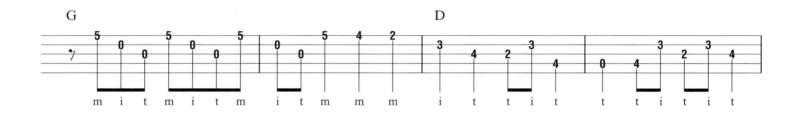

Banjo/Guitar Solo

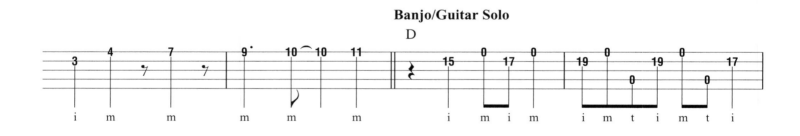

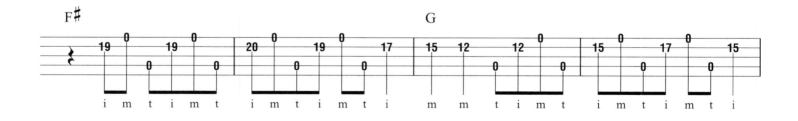

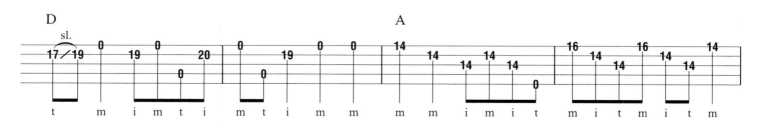

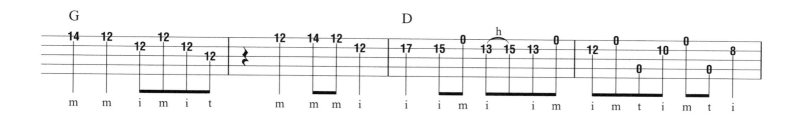

Verse
3. I   left   you   be...

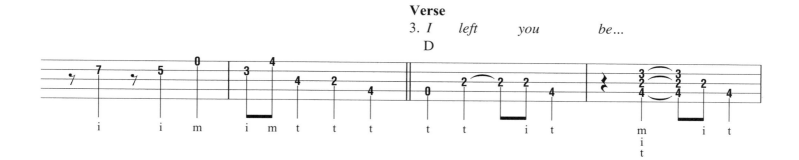

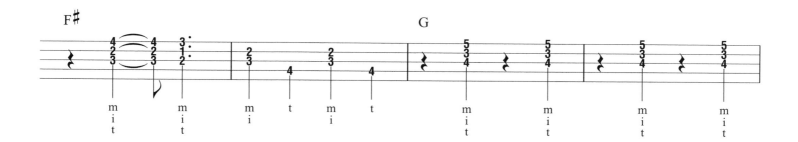

Don't   forget   the flowers...

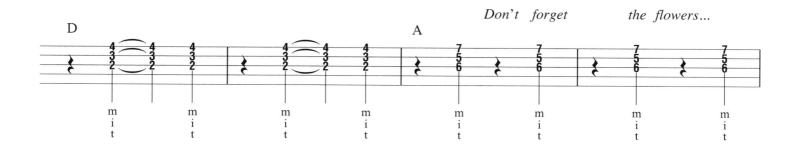

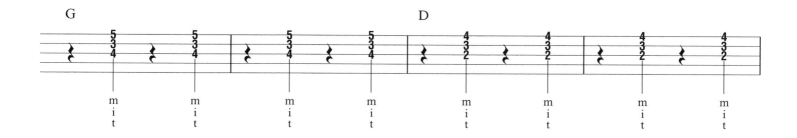

Verse
4. Tryin'   my   patience...

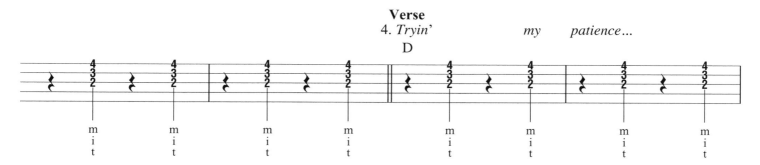

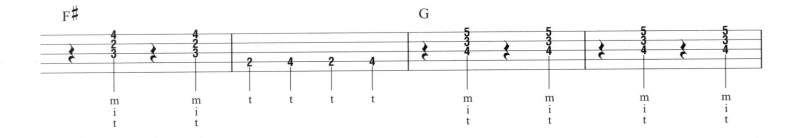

Don't forget the flowers...

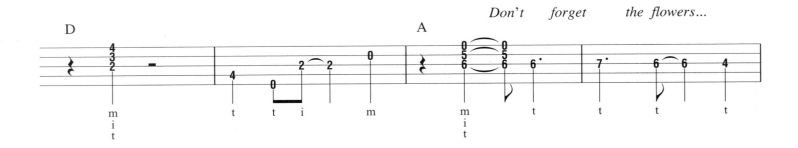

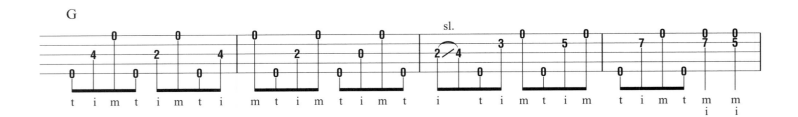

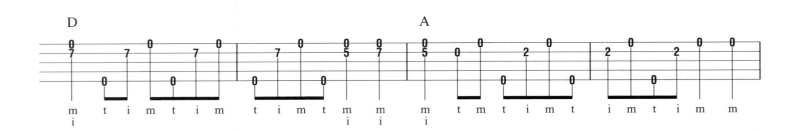

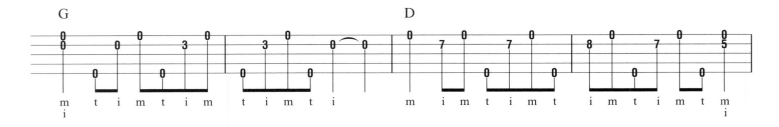

Outro

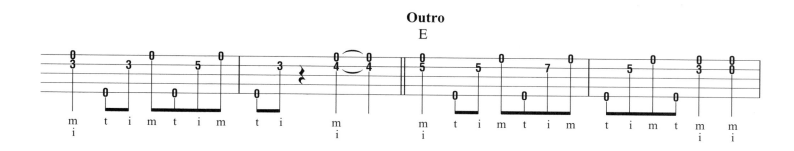

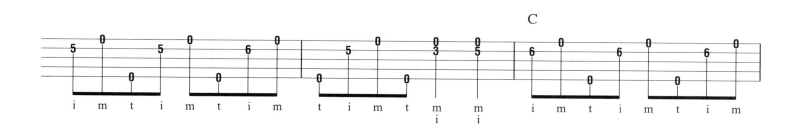

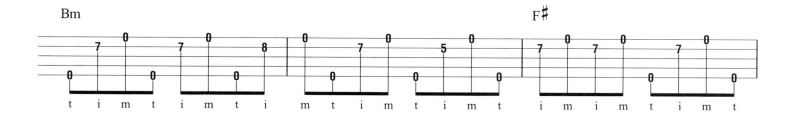

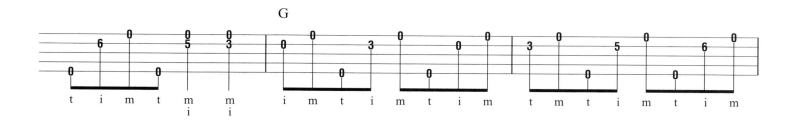

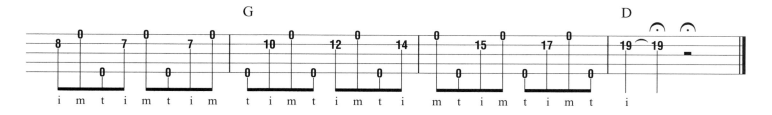

Ho Hey

Words and Music by Jeremy Fraites and Wesley Schultz

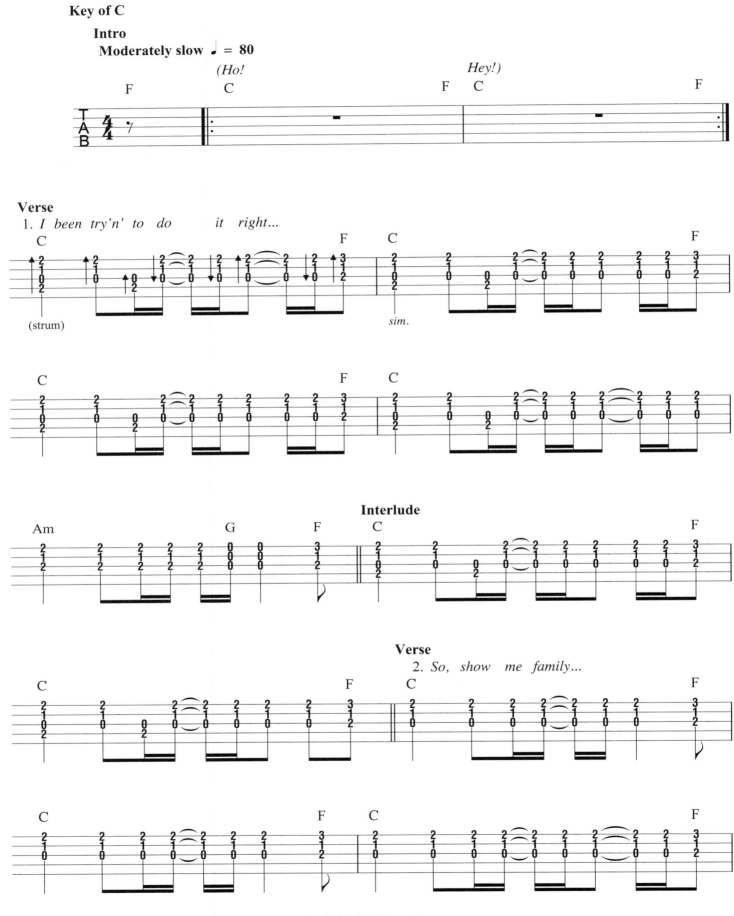

Copyright © 2011 The Lumineers
All Rights Exclusively Administered by Songs Of Kobalt Music Publishing
All Rights Reserved   Used by Permission

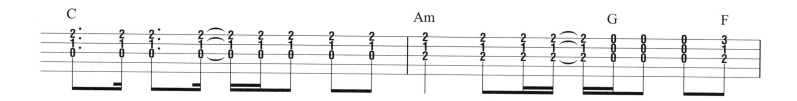

Chorus

I belong with   you,   you belong with   me...

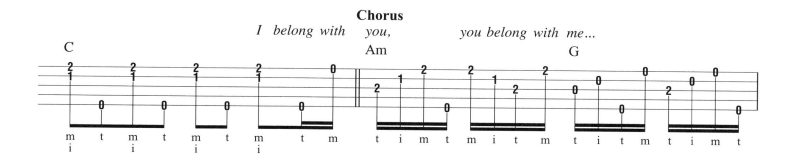

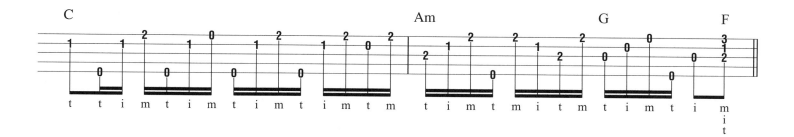

Interlude

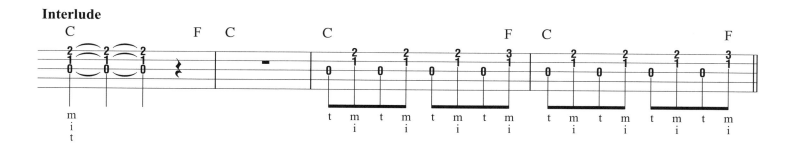

Verse

3. I don't think you're right   for him...

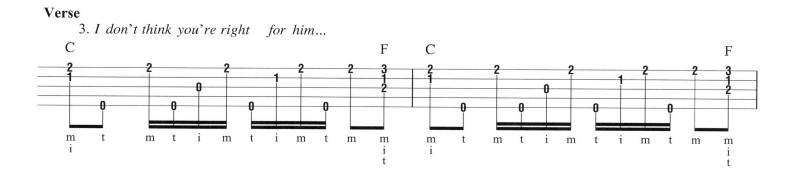

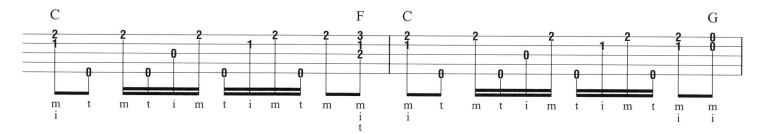

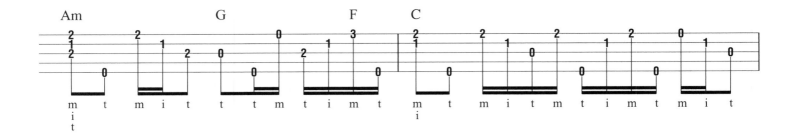

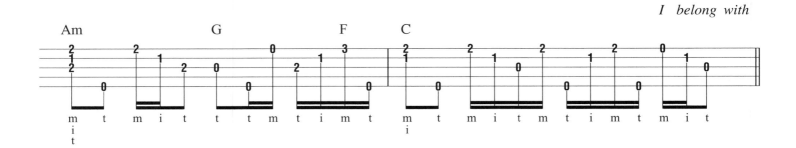

I belong with

Chorus

you,   you belong with me...

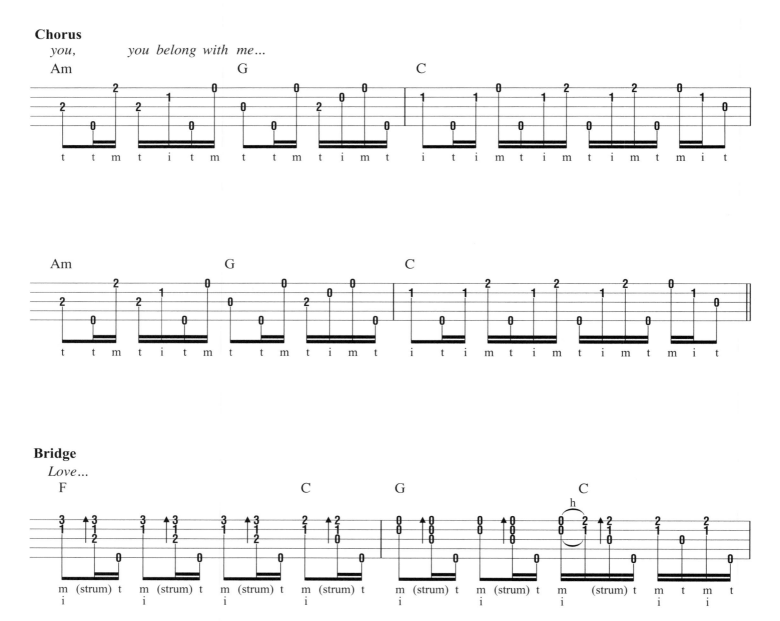

Bridge

Love...

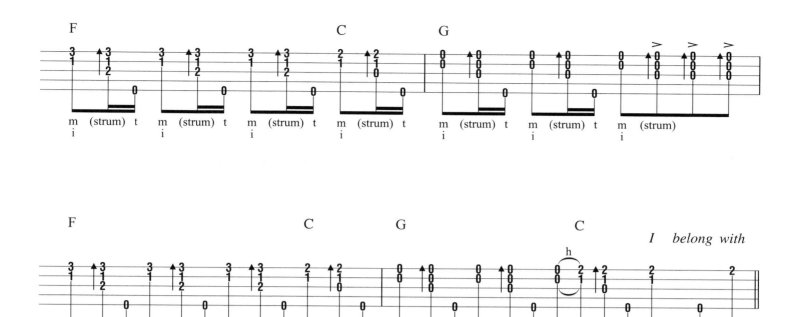

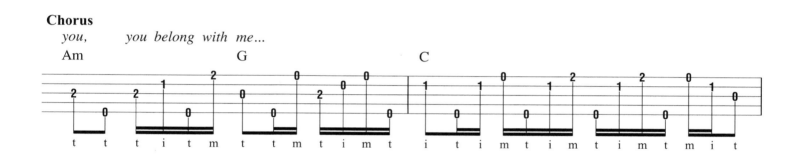

I belong with

Chorus
you,   you belong with me...

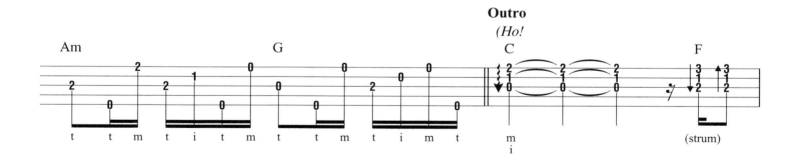

Outro
(Ho!

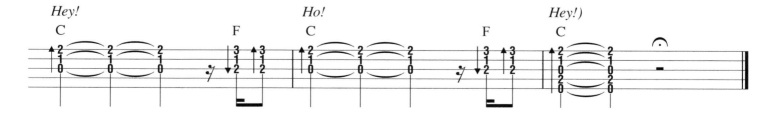

Hey!   *Ho!*   *Hey!)*

from Mumford & Sons - *Sigh No More*

Little Lion Man

Words and Music by Mumford & Sons

Key of F

Tuning, capo III (capo 1st 4 strings only)
(5th-1st) A-D-G-B-D

Intro

Moderately fast ♩ = 80

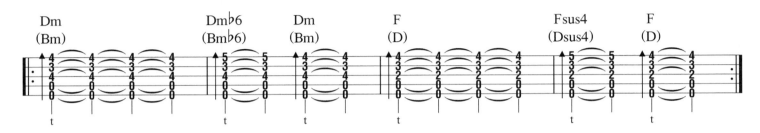

Verse

1. *Weep   for yourself my man,...*

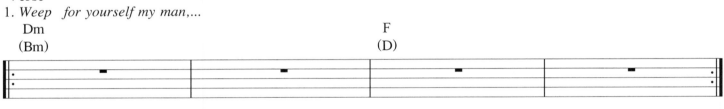

1.   2.

But it was

Chorus

not   your   fault   but   mine...

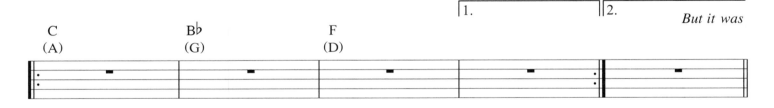

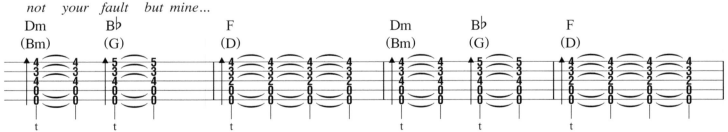

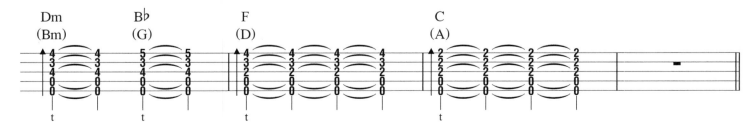

Copyright © 2009 UNIVERSAL MUSIC PUBLISHING LTD.
All Rights in the U.S. and Canada Controlled and Administered by UNIVERSAL - POLYGRAM INTERNATIONAL TUNES, INC.
All Rights Reserved   Used by Permission

Interlude

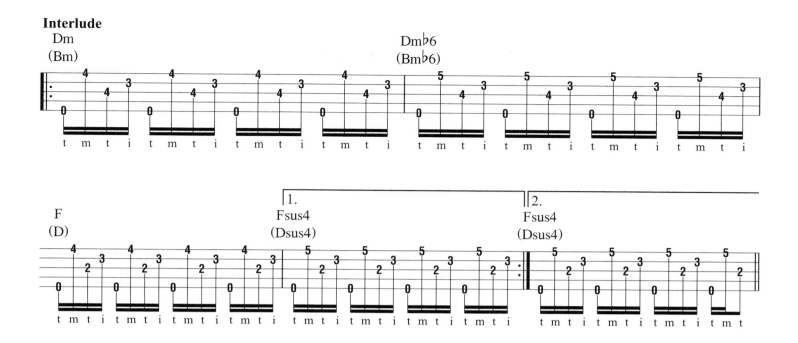

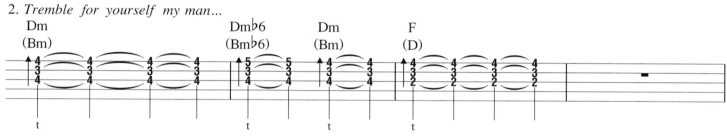

Verse

2. Tremble for yourself my man...

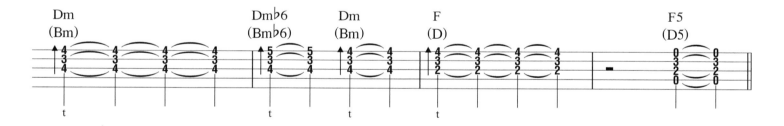

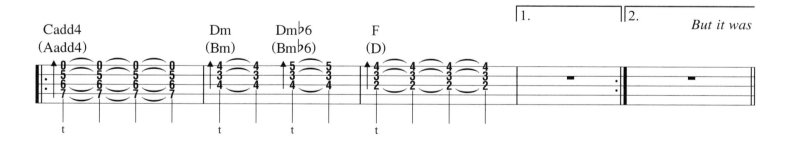

But it was

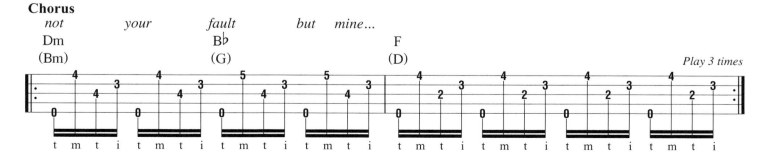

Chorus

not your fault but mine...

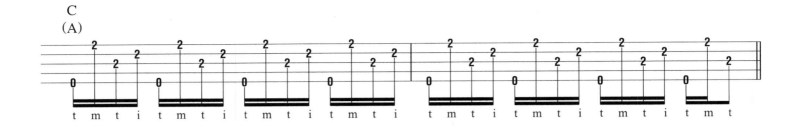

C
(A)

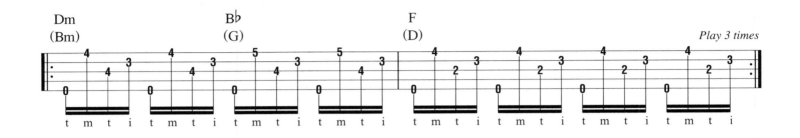

Dm
(Bm)　　　　Bb
　　　　　　(G)　　　　F
　　　　　　　　　　　　(D)　　　　*Play 3 times*

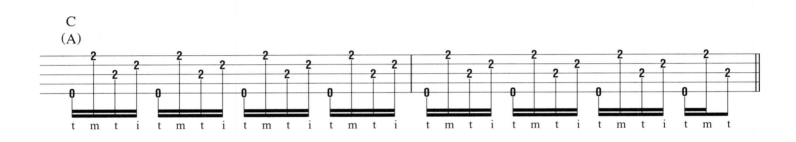

C
(A)

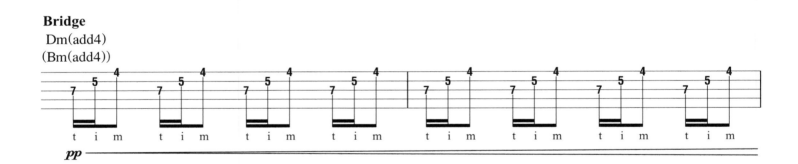

Bridge

Dm(add4)
(Bm(add4))

pp

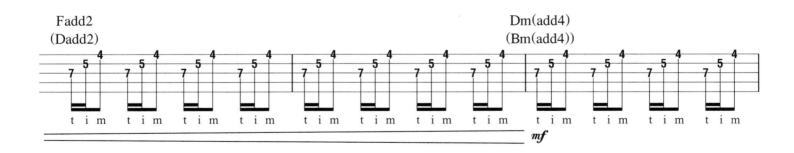

Fadd2
(Dadd2)　　　　　　　　　　　　Dm(add4)
　　　　　　　　　　　　　　　　(Bm(add4))

mf

Fadd2
(Dadd2)

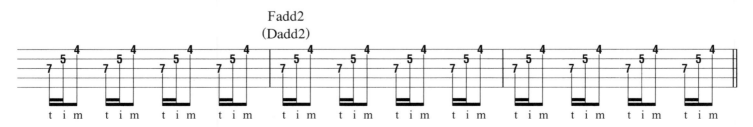

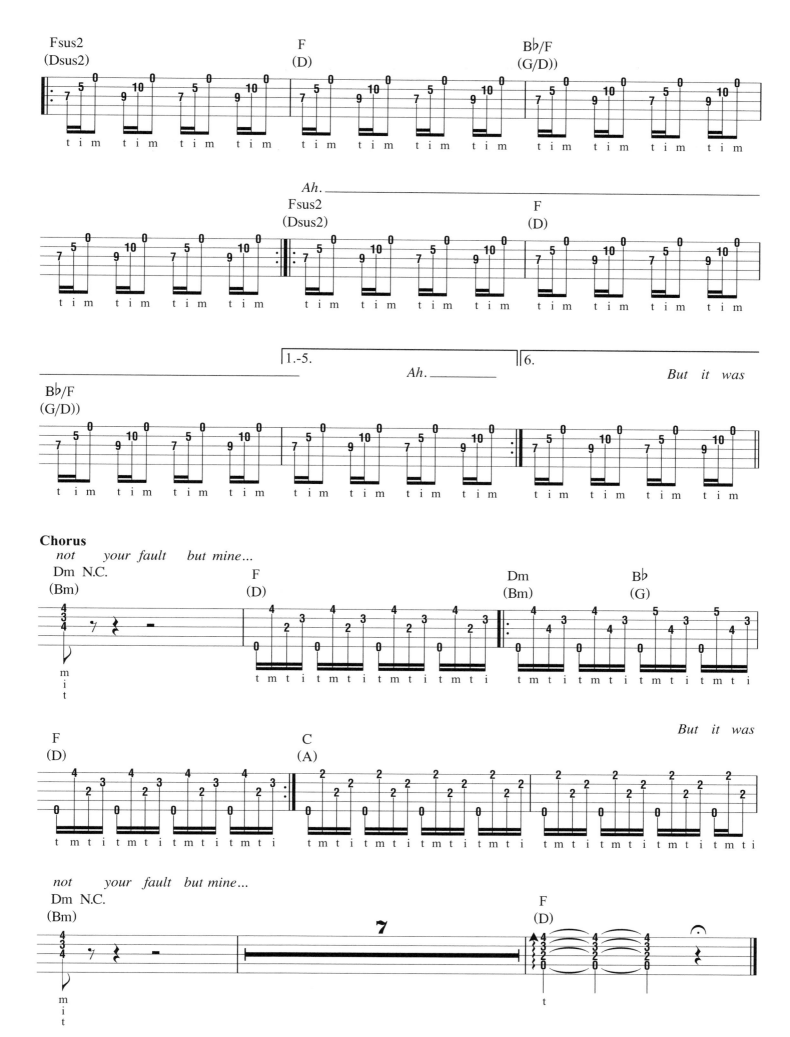

from The Avett Brothers - *The Carpenter*

Live and Die

Words and Music by Scott Avett, Seth Avett and Robert Crawford

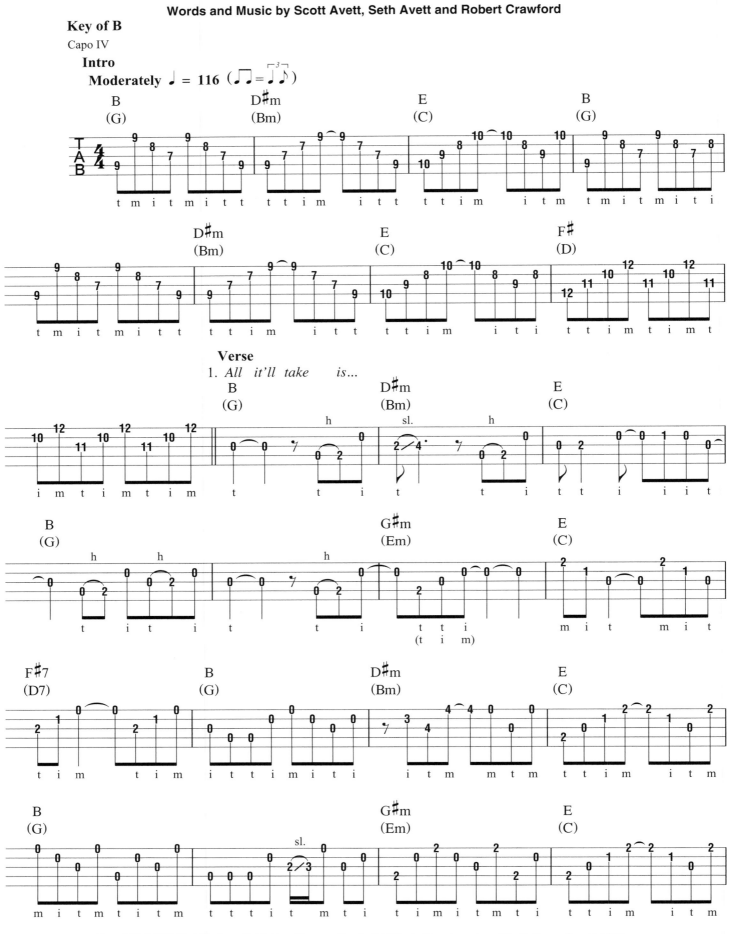

Copyright © 2012 First Big Snow Publishing, Ramseur Family Fold Music, Nemoivmusic and Truth Comes True Publishing
All Rights Administered by BMG Rights Management (US) LLC
All Rights Reserved   Used by Permission

Pre-Chorus

And I wanna love you and more...

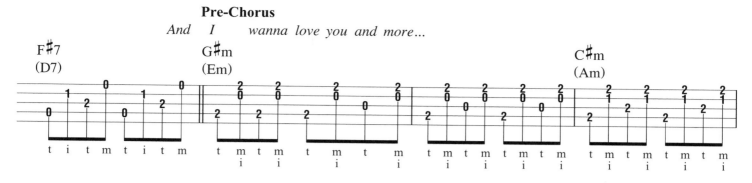

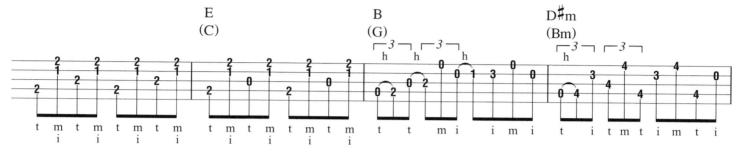

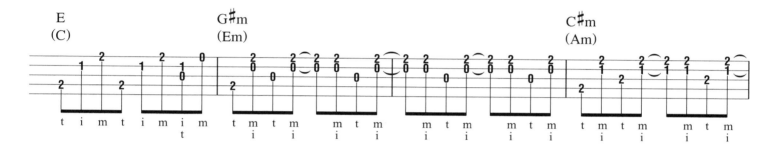

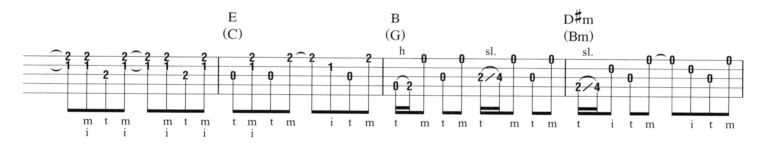

Chorus

You and I, we're the same...

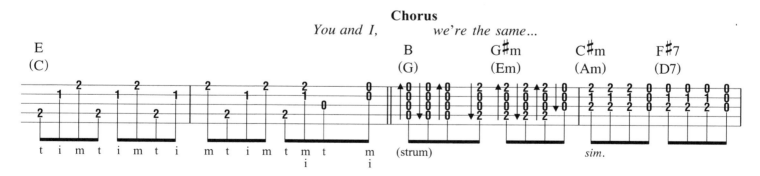

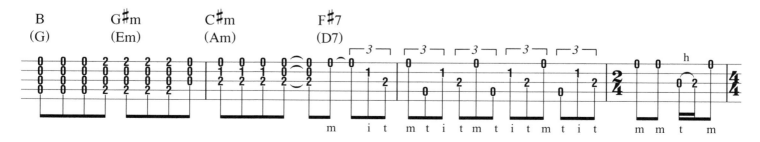

Verse

2. Live like   a Pharoah...

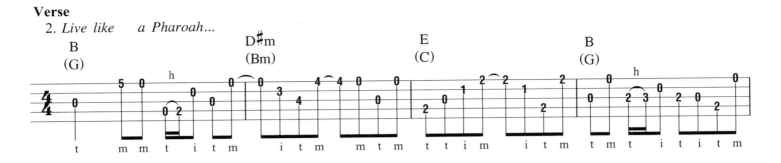

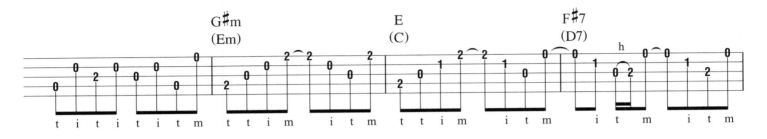

And

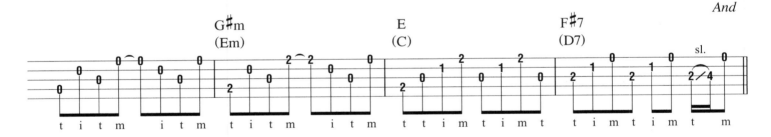

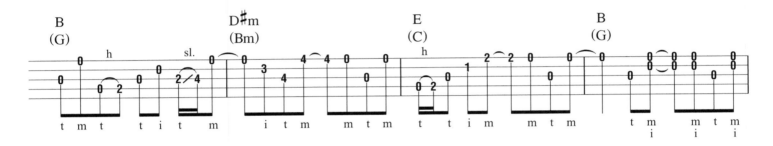

Pre-Chorus

I   wanna love you and more...

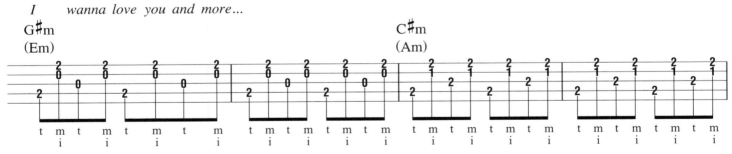

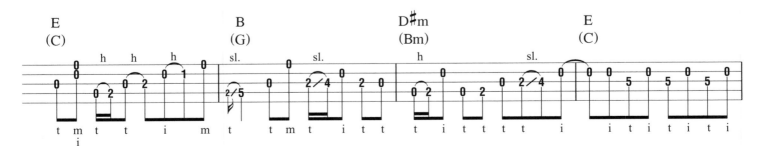

Chorus

You and I,   we're the same...

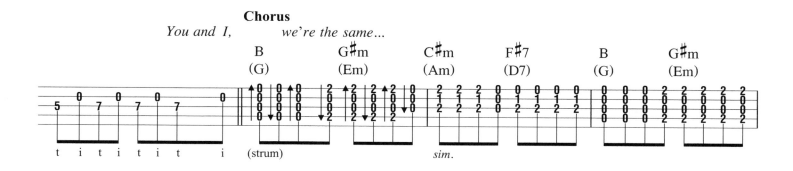

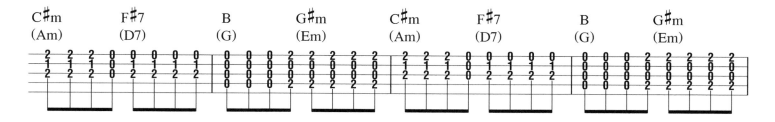

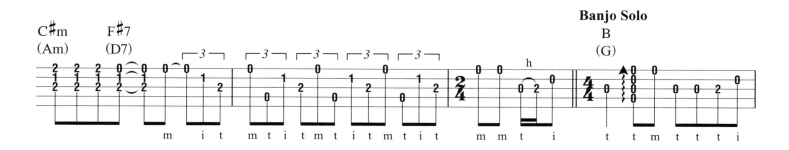

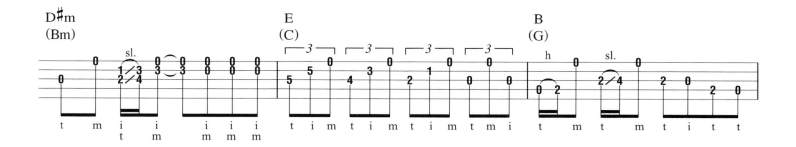

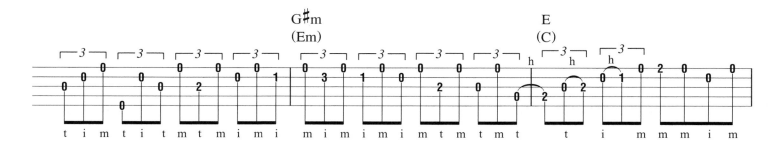

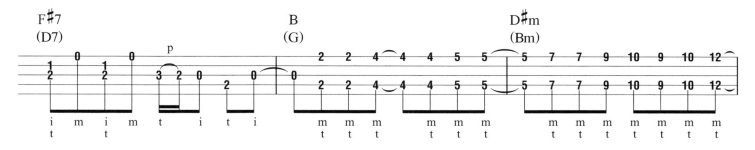

E
(C)

B
(G)

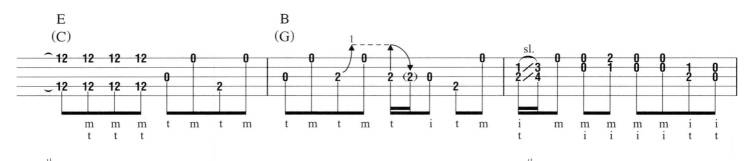

G#m
(Em)

E
(C)

F#7
(D7)

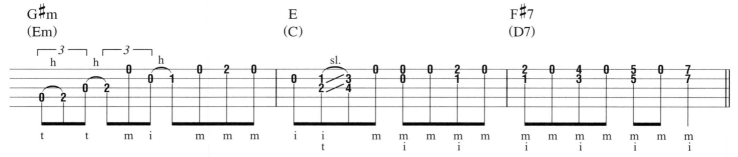

Pre-Chorus

I wanna love you and more...

G#m
(Em)

C#m
(Am)

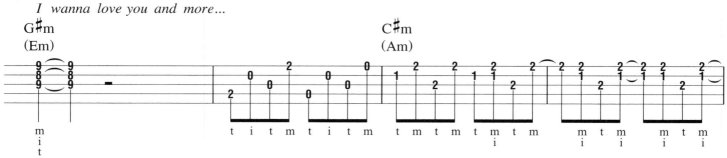

E
(C)

B
(G)

D#m
(Bm)

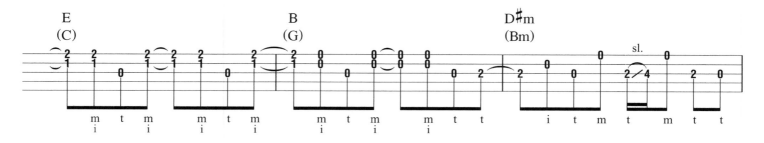

E
(C)

G#m
(Em)

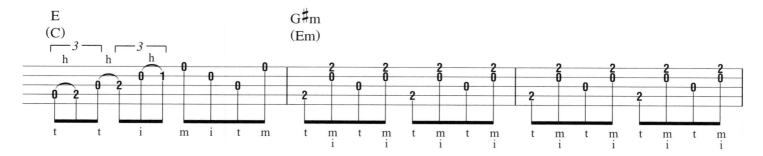

C#m
(Am)

E
(C)

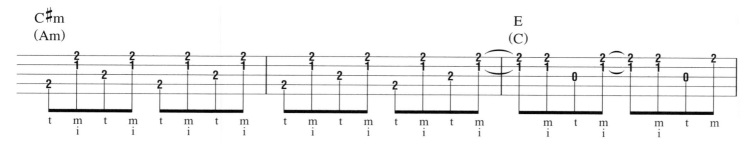

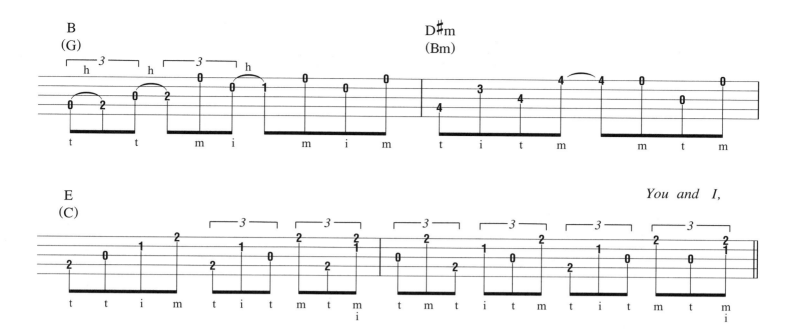

E
(C)

You and I,

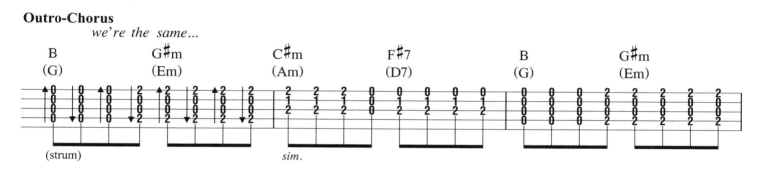

Outro-Chorus

we're the same...

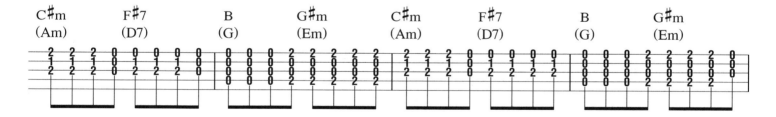

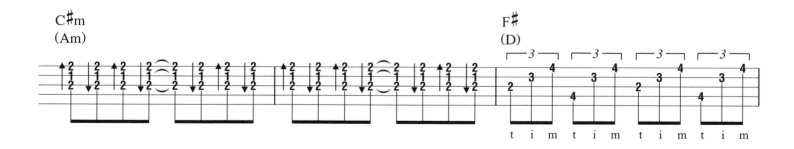

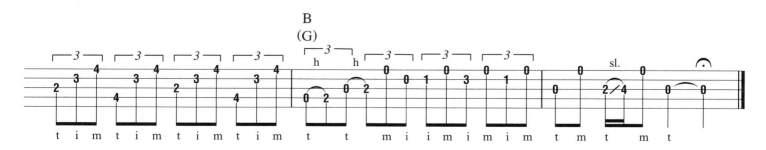

from The Last Bison - *Quill*

Switzerland

Words and Music by Ben Hardesty

Key of E

Capo IX

Intro

Moderately ♩ = 118

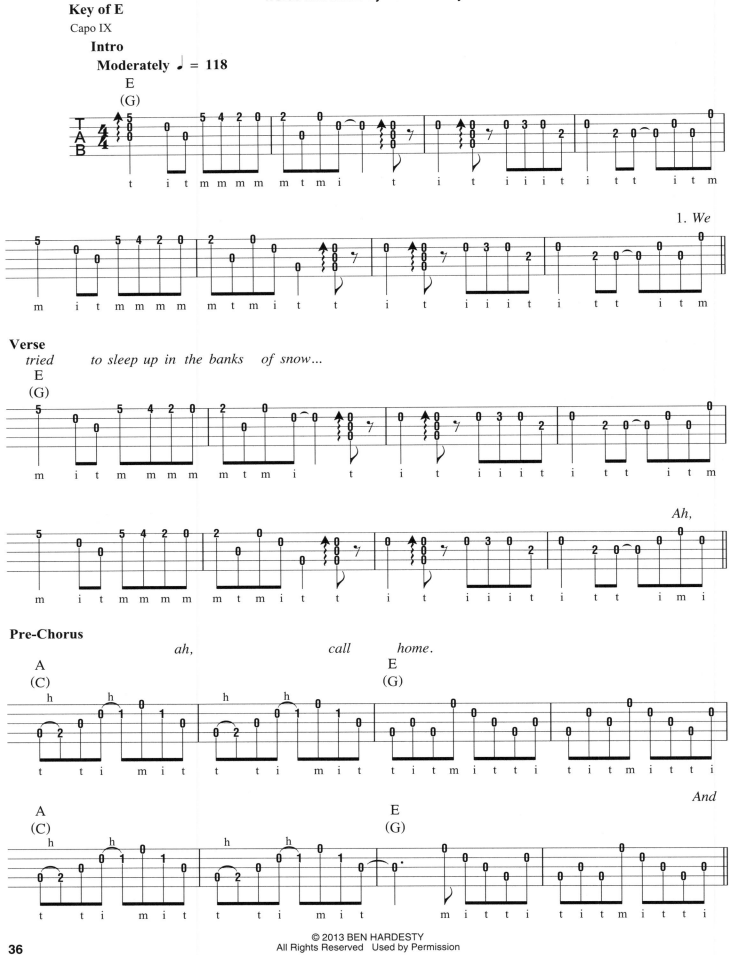

1. We

Verse

tried   to sleep up in the banks   of snow...

Ah,

Pre-Chorus

ah,   call   home.

And

© 2013 BEN HARDESTY
All Rights Reserved   Used by Permission

oh,   oh,   Switzerland...

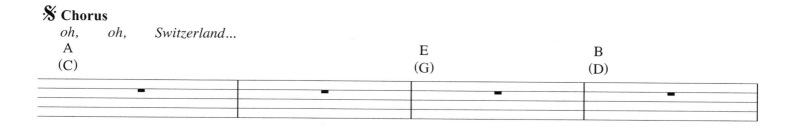

...off the

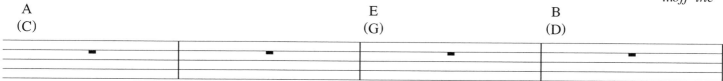

ground.

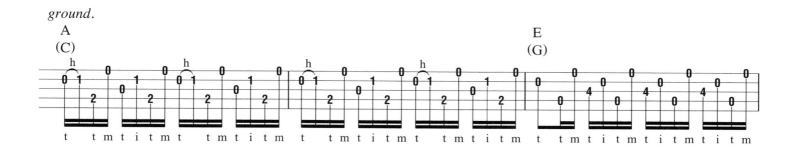

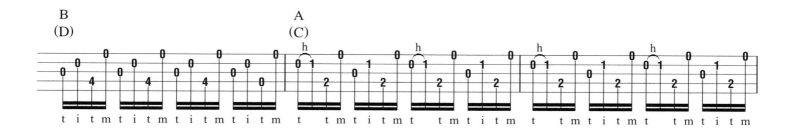

To Coda ⊕

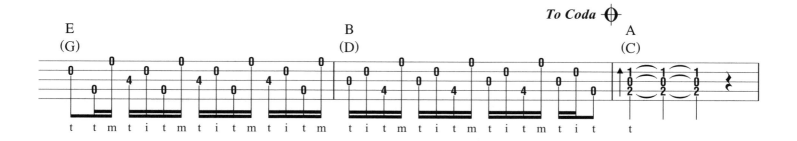

Interlude

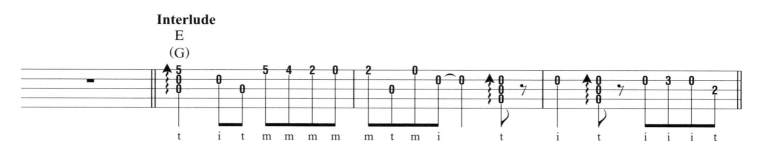

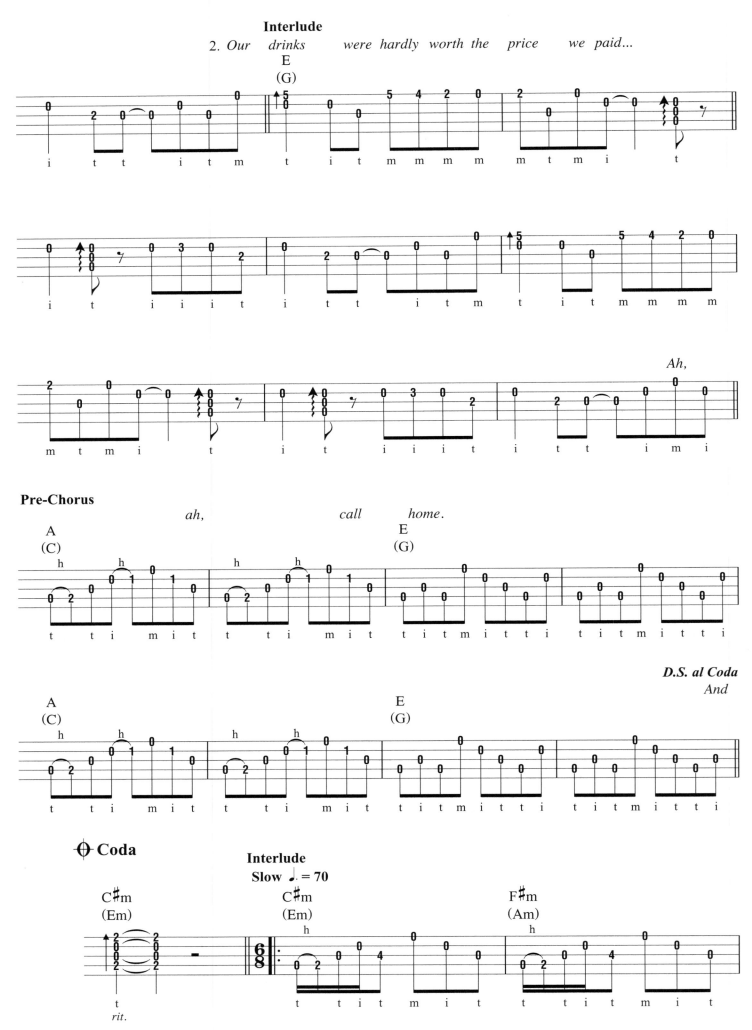

Violin Solo

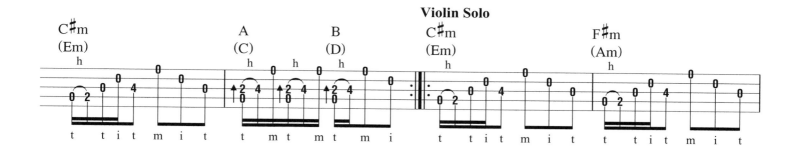

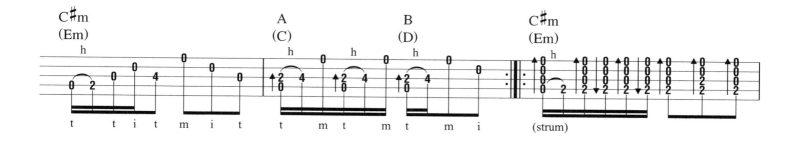

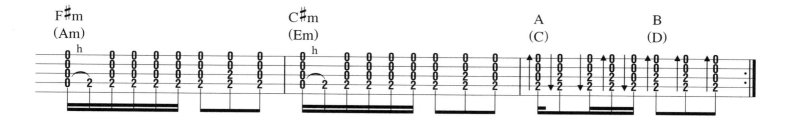

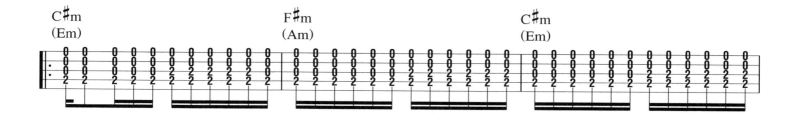

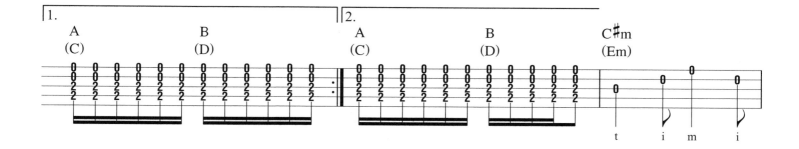

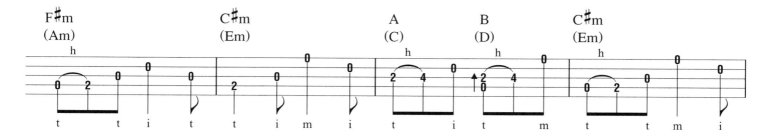

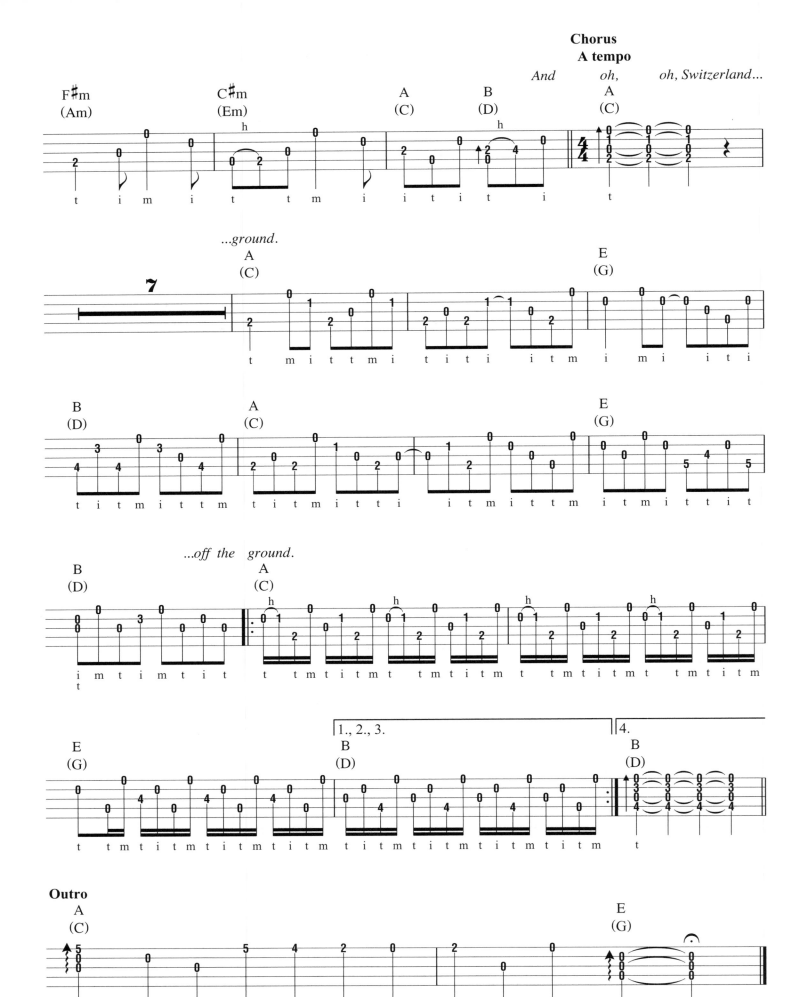

Wagon Wheel

Words and Music by Ketch Secor and Bob Dylan

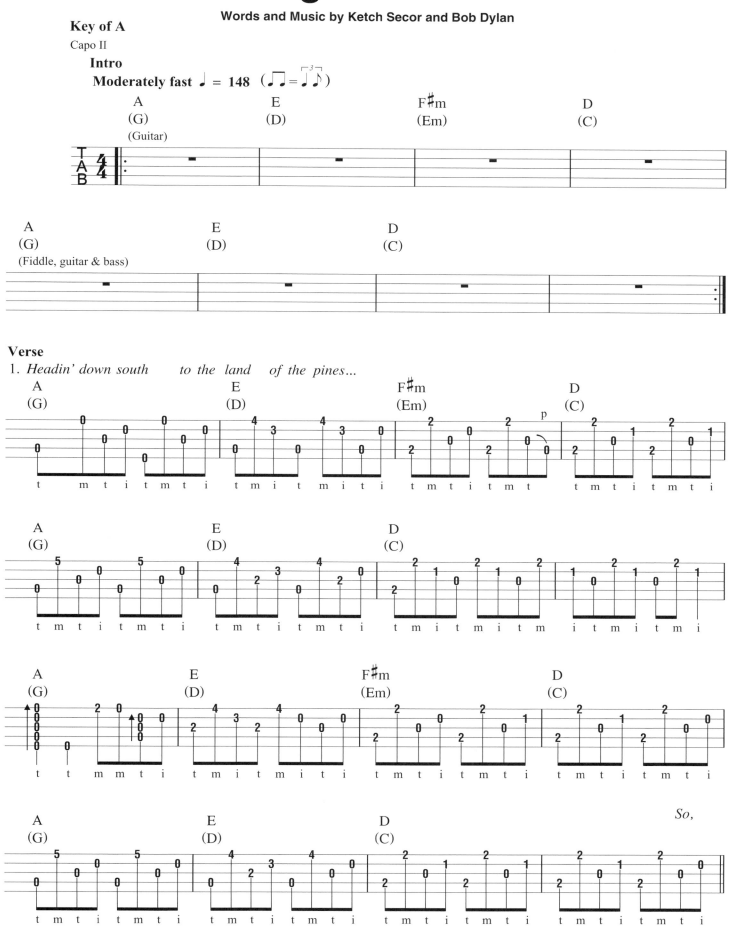

Copyright © 2004 BLOOD DONOR MUSIC and SPECIAL RIDER MUSIC
All Rights for BLOOD DONOR MUSIC Controlled and Administered by SPIRIT ONE MUSIC
International Copyright Secured   All Rights Reserved   Used by Permission

rock   me,   mama, like a   wag - on   wheel...

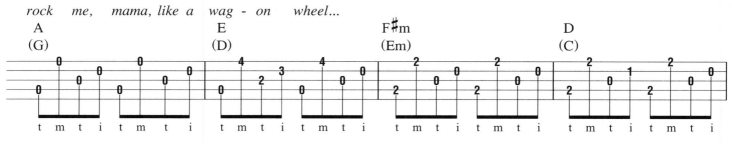

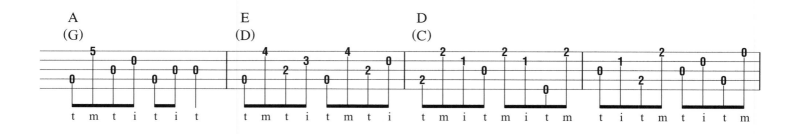

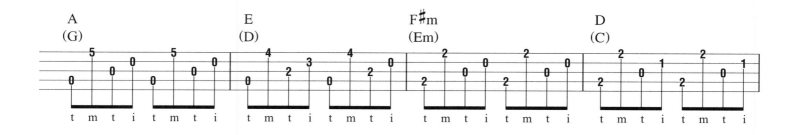

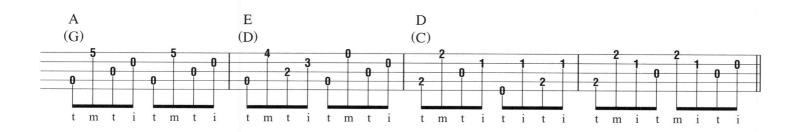

Fiddle Solo

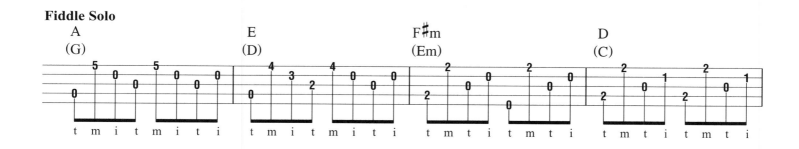

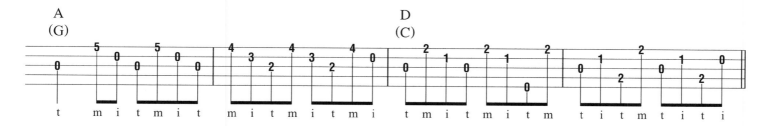

Verse

2. Runnin' from the cold...

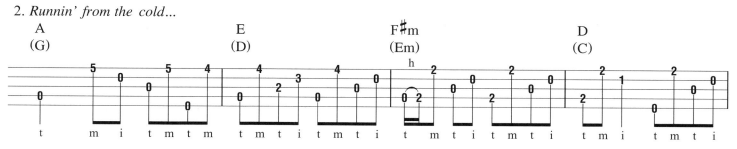

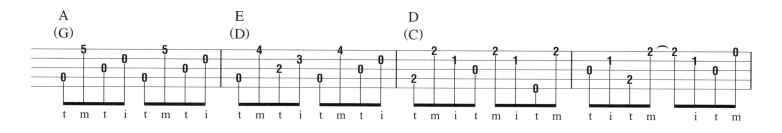

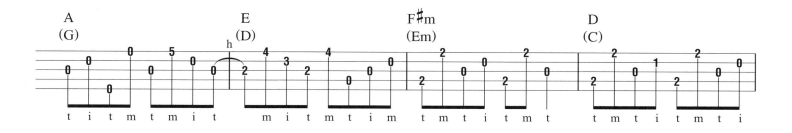

So,

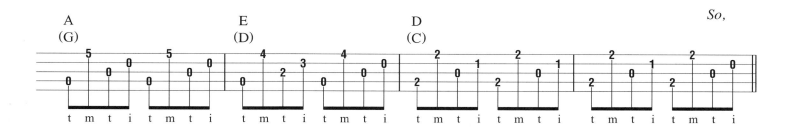

Chorus

rock   me,   mama, like a   wag - on   wheel...

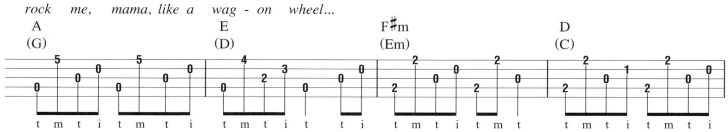

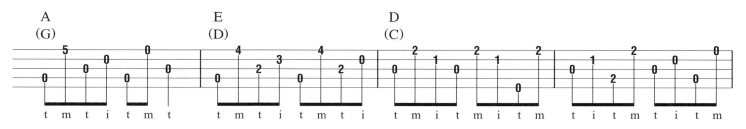

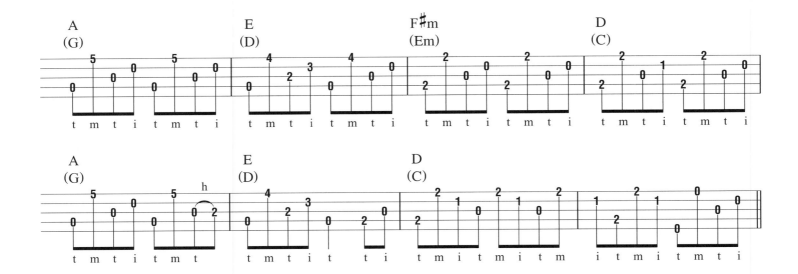

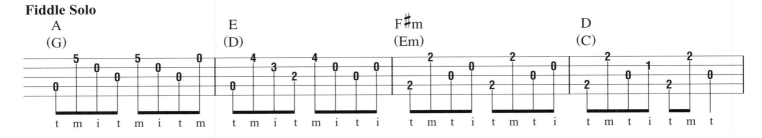

Fiddle Solo

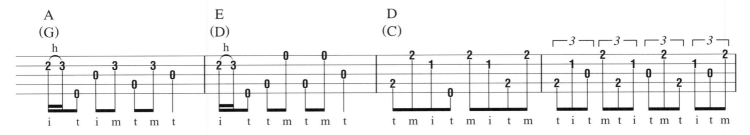

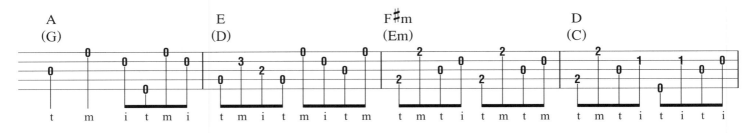

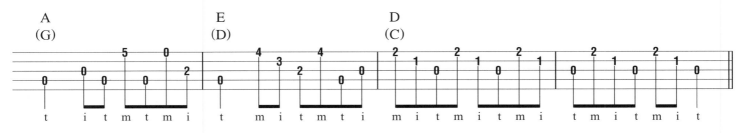

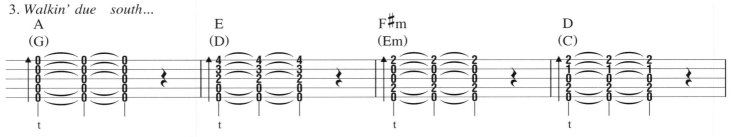

Verse

3. Walkin' due   south…

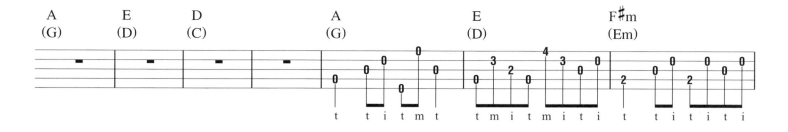

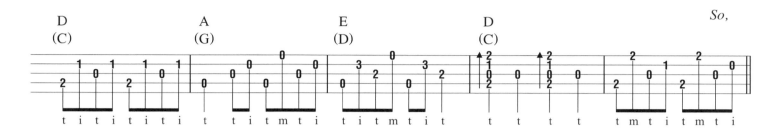

Chorus

rock me, mama, like a wag-on wheel...

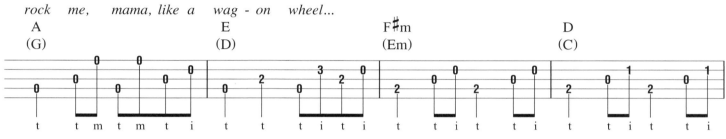

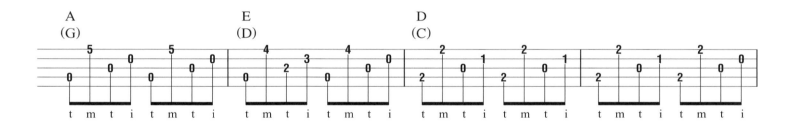

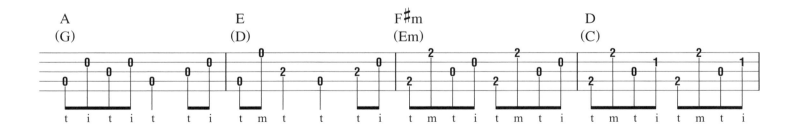

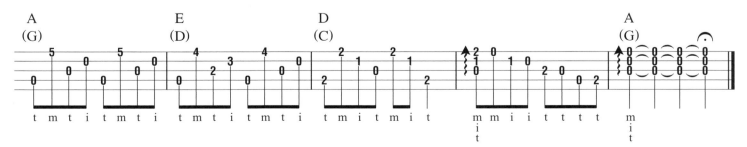

BANJO NOTATION LEGEND

TABLATURE graphically represents the banjo fingerboard. Each horizontal line represents a string, and each number represents a fret.

4th string, 2nd fret   1st & 2nd strings open, played together

TIME SIGNATURE:
The upper number indicates the number of beats per measure, the lower number indicates that a quarter note gets one beat.

CUT TIME:
Each note's time value should be cut in half. As a result, the music will be played twice as fast as it is written.

QUARTER NOTE:
time value = 1 beat

EIGHTH NOTES:
time value = 1/2 beat each

single   in series

SIXTEENTH NOTES:
time value = 1/4 beat each

single   in series

DOTTED QUARTER NOTE:
time value = 1 1/2 beat

TIE: Pick the 1st note only, then let it sustain for the combined time value.

TRIPLET: Three notes played in the same time normally occupied by two notes of the same time value.

GRACE NOTE: A quickly played note with no time value of its own. The grace note and the note following it only occupy the time value of the second note.

RITARD: A gradual slowing of the tempo or speed of the song.

QUARTER REST:
time value = 1 beat of silence

EIGHTH REST:
time value = 1/2 beat of silence

HALF REST:
time value = 2 beats of silence

WHOLE REST:
time value = 4 beats of silence

ENDINGS: When a repeated section has a first and second ending, play the first ending only the first time and play the second ending only the second time.

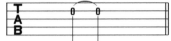

REPEAT SIGNS: Play the music between the repeat signs two times.

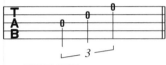

D.S. AL CODA:
Play through the music until you complete the measure labeled *"D.S. al Coda,"* then go back to the sign (𝄋).
Then play until you complete the measure labeled *"To Coda ⊕,"* then skip to the section labeled " ⊕ **Coda.**"

𝄋   *To Coda* ⊕   *D.S. al Coda*   ⊕ *Coda*

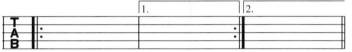

HAMMER-ON: Strike the first (lower) note with one finger, then sound the higher note (on the same string) with another finger by fretting it without picking.

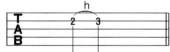

PULL-OFF: Place both fingers on the notes to be sounded. Strike the first note and without picking, pull the finger off to sound the second (lower) note.

SLIDE UP: Strike the first note and then slide the same fret-hand finger up to the second note. The second note is not struck.

SLIDE DOWN: Strike the first note and then slide the same fret-hand finger down to the second note. The second note is not struck.

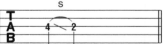

HALF-STEP CHOKE: Strike the note and bend the string up 1/2 step.

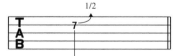

WHOLE-STEP CHOKE: Strike the note and bend the string up one step.

NATURAL HARMONIC: Strike the note while the fret-hand lightly touches the string directly over the fret indicated.

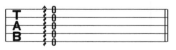

BRUSH: Play the notes of the chord indicated by quickly rolling them from bottom to top.

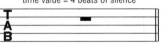

Scruggs/Keith Tuners:

HALF-TWIST UP: Strike the note, twist tuner up 1/2 step, and continue playing.

HALF-TWIST DOWN: Strike the note, twist tuner down 1/2 step, and continue playing.

WHOLE-TWIST UP: Strike the note, twist tuner up one step, and continue playing.

WHOLE-TWIST DOWN: Strike the note, twist tuner down one step, and continue playing.

Right Hand Fingerings

t = thumb   i = index finger   m = middle finger

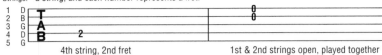

Hal Leonard Banjo Play-Along Series

HAL•LEONARD BANJO PLAY-ALONG

The Banjo Play-Along Series will help you play your favorite songs quickly and easily with incredible backing tracks to help you sound like a bona fide pro! Just follow the banjo tab, listen to the demo track on the CD to hear how the banjo should sound, and then play along with the separate backing tracks. The CD is playable on any CD player and also is enhanced so Mac and PC users can adjust the recording to any tempo without changing the pitch! Each Banjo Play-Along pack features eight cream of the crop songs.

INCLUDES TAB

1. BLUEGRASS
Ashland Breakdown • Deputy Dalton • Dixie Breakdown • Hickory Hollow • I Wish You Knew • I Wonder Where You Are Tonight • Love and Wealth • Salt Creek.
00102585 Book/CD Pack.....................$14.99

2. COUNTRY
East Bound and Down • Flowers on the Wall • Gentle on My Mind • Highway 40 Blues • If You've Got the Money (I've Got the Time) • Just Because • Take It Easy • You Are My Sunshine.
00105278 Book/CD Pack.....................$14.99

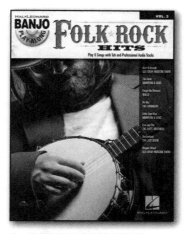

3. FOLK/ROCK HITS
Ain't It Enough • The Cave • Forget the Flowers • Ho Hey • Little Lion Man • Live and Die • Switzerland • Wagon Wheel.
00119867 Book/CD Pack.....................$14.99

4. OLD-TIME CHRISTMAS
Away in a Manger • Hark! the Herald Angels Sing • Jingle Bells • Joy to the World • O Holy Night • O Little Town of Bethlehem • Silent Night • We Wish You a Merry Christmas.
00119889 Book/CD Pack.....................$14.99

HAL•LEONARD® CORPORATION

7777 W. BLUEMOUND RD. P.O. BOX 13819 MILWAUKEE, WI 53213

www.halleonard.com

Prices, contents, and availability subject to change without notice.

0614

GREAT BANJO PUBLICATIONS

FROM HAL LEONARD CORPORATION

Hal Leonard Banjo Method – Second Edition

by Mac Robertson, Robbie Clement, Will Schmid
This innovative method teaches 5-string banjo bluegrass style using a carefully paced approach that keeps beginners playing great songs *while learning.* Book 1 covers easy chord strums, tablature, right-hand rolls, hammer-ons, slides and pull-offs, and more. Book 2 includes solos and licks, fiddle tunes, back-up, capo use, and more.

00699500 Book 1 (Book Only)..................... $7.99
00695101 Book 1 (Book/CD Pack)............................ $16.99
00699502 Book 2 (Book Only...................... $7.99

Banjo Chord Finder

This extensive reference guide covers over 2,800 banjo chords, including four of the most commonly used tunings. Thirty different chord qualities are covered for each key, and each chord quality is presented in two different voicings. Also includes a lesson on chord construction and a fingerboard chart of the banjo neck!

00695741 9 x 12.. $6.99
00695742 6 x 9.. $5.95

Banjo Scale Finder

by Chad Johnson
Learn to play scales on the banjo with this comprehensive yet easy-to-use book. It contains more than 1,300 scale diagrams for the most often-used scales and modes, including multiple patterns for each scale. Also includes a lesson on scale construction and a fingerboard chart of the banjo neck.

00695780 9 x 12.. $6.95
00695783 6 x 9.. $5.95

The Beatles for Banjo

18 of the Fab Four's finest for five string banjo! Includes: Across the Universe • Blackbird • A Hard Day's Night • Here Comes the Sun • Hey Jude • Let It Be • She Loves You • Strawberry Fields Forever • Ticket to Ride • Yesterday • and more.

00700813 ....$14.99

Christmas Favorites for Banjo

27 holiday classics arranged for banjo, including: Blue Christmas • Feliz Navidad • Frosty the Snow Man • Grandma's Killer Fruitcake • A Holly Jolly Christmas • I Saw Mommy Kissing Santa Claus • It's Beginning to Look like Christmas • Jingle-Bell Rock • Nuttin' for Christmas • Rudolph the Red-Nosed Reindeer • Silver Bells • and more.

00699109.. $10.95

Fretboard Roadmaps

by Fred Sokolow
This handy book/CD pack will get you playing all over the banjo fretboard in any key! You'll learn to: increase your chord, scale and lick vocabulary • play chord-based licks, moveable major and blues scales, melodic scales and first-position major scales • and much more! The CD includes 51 demonstrations of the exercises.

00695358 Book/CD Pack $14.95

O Brother, Where Art Thou?

Banjo tab arrangements of 12 bluegrass/folk songs from this Grammy-winning album. Includes: The Big Rock Candy Mountain • Down to the River to Pray • I Am a Man of Constant Sorrow • I Am Weary (Let Me Rest) • I'll Fly Away • In the Jailhouse Now • Keep on the Sunny Side • You Are My Sunshine • and more, plus lyrics and a banjo notation legend.

00699528 Banjo Tablature...................... $12.95

Earl Scruggs and the 5-String Banjo

Earl Scruggs' legendary method has helped thousands of banjo players get their start. It features everything you need to know to start playing, even how to build your own banjo! Topics covered include: Scruggs tuners • how to read music • chords • how to read tablature • anatomy of Scruggs-style picking • exercises in picking • 44 songs • biographical notes • and more! The CD features Earl Scruggs playing and explaining over 60 examples!

00695764 Book Only.................................. $19.95
00695765 Book/CD Pack $34.99

The Tony Trischka Collection

59 authentic transcriptions by Tony Trischka, one of the world's best banjo pickers and instructors. Includes: Blown Down Wall • China Grove • Crossville Breakdown • Heartlands • Hill Country • Kentucky Bullfight • A Robot Plane Flies over Arkansas • and more. Features an introduction by Béla Fleck, plus Tony's comments on each song. Transcriptions are in tab only.

00699063 Banjo Tablature........................ $19.95

The Ultimate Banjo Songbook

A great collection of banjo classics: Alabama Jubilee • Bye Bye Love • Duelin' Banjos • The Entertainer • Foggy Mountain Breakdown • Great Balls of Fire • Lady of Spain • Orange Blossom Special • (Ghost) Riders in the Sky • Rocky Top • San Antonio Rose • Tennessee Waltz • UFO-TOFU • You Are My Sunshine • and more.

00699565 Book/2-CD Pack $24.95

FOR MORE INFORMATION, SEE YOUR LOCAL MUSIC DEALER, OR WRITE TO:

HAL•LEONARD®
CORPORATION
7777 W. BLUEMOUND RD. P.O. BOX 13819 MILWAUKEE, WI 53213

Prices, contents, and availability subject to change without notice.

Visit Hal Leonard online at **www.halleonard.com**

0514